THE DESERT
VET

ALEX TINSON has lived and worked in the United Arab Emirates as a vet for nearly thirty years.

DAVID HARDAKER is a former ABC Middle East correspondent and a Walkley Award winning journalist. He has lived and worked for many years in the Arab world and speaks Arabic.

THE DESERT VET

How a city boy became a Bedouin nomad
and spent thirty years caring for a menagerie
of camels and other exotic creatures

ALEX TINSON
WITH DAVID HARDAKER

ALLEN&UNWIN
SYDNEY • MELBOURNE • AUCKLAND • LONDON

First published in 2016

Allen & Unwin
83 Alexander Street
Crows Nest NSW 2065
Australia
Phone: (61 2) 8425 0100
Email: info@allenandunwin.com
Web: www.allenandunwin.com

Cataloguing-in-Publication details are available
from the National Library of Australia
www.trove.nla.gov.au

ISBN 978 1 76029 282 9

Set in 11.5/15.5 pt Sabon by Midland Typesetters, Australia

10 9 8 7 6 5 4 3 2 1

*To my mother Catherine Tinson . . . who gave me the inner
strength to deal with my darker moments . . . and always
managed to ground me when I got too carried away . . .*
Alex Tinson

*To my wife Bronwen and our boys Sel and Jesse, thank you
for your endless love and support.*

*My gratitude also to Richard Walsh, Rebecca Kaiser and
Simone Ford for your huge encouragement and calm
professionalism.*

*Finally, I wish to dedicate this book to the memory of
my great friend Mohamed Serour, who opened the Arabic
language and the Arab world to me through countless
coffee-fuelled sessions in the cafes of Alexandria and Cairo.
What a tragedy that you never lived in freedom.*
David Hardaker

Contents

One
Camel tragic

The sheikhs of Abu Dhabi and Dubai, amongst the wealthiest men in the world, are gathered together. Dressed in crisp white cotton robes, they've taken their seats on plush red, gold-edged chairs. The royal box is festooned with flowers of a dozen hues and filled with the scent of magnolia and roses.

The seating is a study in itself, a pecking order of who holds power in the oil-rich sheikhdom of the United Arab Emirates. The Abu Dhabi royal family is first, Dubai's royal family second. It's a reflection of where centuries of tribal history and conflict have led them.

These rulers of modern Arabia are at peace, but still in a kind of war. Now their rivalry is being played out in a traditional setting, the camel races. It's a clash of cultures within a culture: the dust, sand and sweat of a desert contest set against the gleaming Rolex watches and Maseratis of the sheikhs. The past in the present.

Today, pride is on the line. Dubai's ruler might have the world's shiniest tall towers and biggest shopping malls and he might have attracted global brands to his glittering city. By contrast the ruler of Abu Dhabi is a study in quiet power. He is the supreme leader, the President of the United Arab Emirates, and in his hands lie ten per cent of the world's known oil reserves. Everyone knows it.

At stake is the winner's prize, the prestigious Golden Sword—an Arab symbol of power and wealth which is handed to the race—plus hundreds of thousands of dollars in cash and cars. But this race is about much more: this is a contest for tribal supremacy in an ancient art. For all their wealth, all their Bentleys and Ferraris and golden palaces, what matters is who wins this contest and who owns the fastest camel.

In this inner sanctum of Arabia there is one outsider. My mission has been to make the president's camels the fastest in the Gulf and I am here to carry out last-minute checks on my animals. This is the culmination of close to three decades' work, a professional life spent as the keeper of the president's camels, using my science to make his animals faster, bigger, stronger. Success has made me the world's leading camel vet. And it's brought me inside the fabulously wealthy but rarely glimpsed world of the Arab sheikhs.

Camels brought me here and they have kept me here for half my life.

■   ■   ■

I am a full-blown camel tragic.

If you sit in the still desert sands and wait quietly, camels will approach, curious to know more of who you are and what you are up to. Camels are herd animals and they are incredibly vocal. They make sounds that seem scary and nasty to people who don't know them, but really they are just talking to each other. It is a language I've learned and as I move through the herd I mimic the male's low, grunting call, made by blowing through flapping lips to produce a bubbling sound. If a female raises her tail it tells me she is already pregnant. If not then she is ready to be mated.

I am at home in the company of camels. Where others see a dirty, filthy, smelly, kicking, spitting beast, I see a thing of pure anatomical beauty, an intelligent and graceful creature that is perfectly adapted to its environment. I see a magnificent animal that comes in various shapes and hues, from the slender and powerful brown racing camel that is capable of galloping at speeds above forty kilometres an hour, to the resplendent and huge black camel that fetches millions of dollars in local 'beauty' contests.

My house is a private shrine to camels. As I look around there's a picture of my daughters with the cutest baby camels you've ever seen. There's a two-humped camel carved out of a tree root by a Mongolian tribesman. Next to it is a camel fashioned out of a piece of four-and-a-half-billion-year-old meteorite. I keep framed photos of my camels on sideboards and atop my desk as others keep photos of their families.

Professionally, my role is chief vet for the racing camels of the President of the United Arab Emirates and Ruler of Abu Dhabi, His Royal Highness Sheikh Khalifa bin Zayed. The research centre we started thirty years ago has been a global pioneer in embryo transfer technology and has produced half a dozen world firsts.

I also have my own collection of camels including, at the moment, three new babies. Apart from anything else, they're good fun.

This is my game. This is what I do.

Living where I do, camels have helped me merge with the Bedouin of Arabia. In times of personal grief, I have retreated to the world of camels and found comfort there. Because of camels I have gone from rags to riches, then to rags and finally back to riches again.

It's definitely an obsession, and one that has led me to live close to half my life in a town called Al Ain in the United Arab Emirates. Thirty years ago I'd never heard of it. Now I would never leave it.

The United Arab Emirates is famous for Dubai's spiralling towers and mega shopping malls. It's a magnet for westerners who are looking for a fix of Arabia, done in luxury. Alternatively, it's a tax-free, high-salary haven where Australians, the British and Americans come for a life-changing income—and then invariably leave after three or four years.

I've seen thousands of visitors come and go and have known a fair share of them. But I've stayed, on and on and on. In that time I've witnessed an extreme pace of development, perhaps unparalleled in the history of the world, as their society has transformed from a poor desert existence to an ultra-modern state.

Now, as the grandfather of Emirati children, I am also tied to this world by blood.

Because of camels I have built a life I never imagined possible. And it all happened because I decided to say yes to adventure whenever it came my way.

■ ■ ■

Camels might be my grand obsession but they were not my first. I say 'obsession' rather than 'love' because it's hard to love these animals of the wild. They're not cute and cuddly. They don't roll over on command or fetch a stick or jump on your lap. For me they have something else: they offer the lure of freedom and danger. It's an intoxicating mix and it lets you know you are alive.

You could say it was genetically programmed in me; being

a vet is now a Tinson tradition. In my extended family I can count more than twenty of us who are vets. My brother's a vet. His daughter is a vet. My sister's married to a vet whose brothers are vets. On and on and on it goes. Some of them work on farms. Some run veterinary clinics.

But much as I appreciate the value of their work, I never wanted to be the family vet down the road, looking after Mr and Mrs Smith's cat with the runny nose. From as early as I can remember I've been drawn, by instinct, to the exotic and the dangerous.

I grew up in St Ives, the sort of Sydney suburb that produces lawyers, bankers and doctors. It was a white bread, neat-as-a-pin neighbourhood of family cars, big mortgages and grim ambition. But we were also on the outskirts of the city and, lucky for me, our house backed onto bushland and a creek. If you followed that creek for a few kilometres it took you to Ku-ring-gai Chase National Park, a whole other world untouched and untamed by civilisation. In no time at all you could feel you were in the Amazon.

This was my private world and I took every chance to escape to it, sometimes with my mates but usually by myself. When I was alone I felt at one with everything around me. Here was a place I could lose myself for hours at a time. I knew the trees, the rocks and the life that lived within it. If you looked carefully, you could pick out the water dragons, lyre-birds, kangaroos and rock wallabies against the browns and greens of the bush. I learned to move noiselessly along narrow tracks and then hold myself still lest the wildlife sensed me in their midst.

My favourites, though, were the things found hidden under rocks or slipping through the undergrowth, scary little beasts that most people flinch from: the goannas, the lizards and most of all the snakes.

How can you love a snake? The answer is: you can't. But everything about snakes fascinated me. I loved how utterly different they were to any other living being. For me they had an otherworldly quality. They were enigmatic. They were exotic. And it made me feel exotic to own one.

I collected snakes like other kids collected football cards, always trying to catch a bigger one, a rarer one, until I gathered the complete set of species. And of course there was the sheer thrill of the hunt, tracking and then catching something deadly like a tiger snake or a black snake without getting bitten. You needed to be agile, alert and make instant decisions, because it was indeed a matter of life and death.

Bit by bit I turned our suburban home into my own private zoo. It started in my bedroom, which became home to an assorted collection of snakes and other reptiles. One prized possession was my collection of seven baby goannas with their brilliant black and yellow markings, hatched from eggs I'd discovered in a termite nest at the back of the house. They were a rare find and made me the envy of my mates. I traded most of them away but I hung on to the biggest one, called Chopper, who seemed to enjoy playing a weird game with me. While I studied at my desk, Chopper would climb the bookcase, up the wall and then spring onto my head. Again and again.

The pythons I found in the bush became way too big for my room so they went under the house in a special cage that I built. And finally I took over the rumpus room, which not only housed the overflow of lizards and goannas but became my special hiding place for the poisonous snakes I wasn't meant to bring into the house. Mostly I got away with it, though there was the time when the black snake flew for my finger as I was feeding it a lizard. I ended up in intensive care, vomiting and with my arm swollen and blue from the venom. Mum and Dad were generally tolerant of my snake fascination but the episode with the black snake—and finding a tiger snake in my bedroom—pushed my long-suffering Mum and Dad too far. Neither of them was prone to screaming and shouting, but what if it had sunk its fangs into my little sister or brother?

How would I feel then? My pocket money was cut off for three months, and so was my snake collecting.

My animal friends were, in fact, not the least bit friendly. Most of them were actually quite keen on killing me.

For a kid with a vet's blood in his veins, growing up in the sixties and seventies was a great time. There were movies like *Born Free* and books like *My Family and Other Animals* by the wonderful English zookeeper and author Gerald Durrell. They showed me how a life lived amongst the wild things could be so exhilarating. I fancied that I might live life big with animals, just like Gerald Durrell, and wake up with an ocelot or a chameleon for company in my bedroom. I think I knew even then that these wonderful tales were in fact a nicely packaged reality for those who craved a little excitement in their humdrum lives. It was a romantic notion, and it seemed so remote for a kid marooned in the suburbs.

It was around the time I had latched on to my Gerald Durrell fantasy that Dad's work as an industrial chemist took him to South Africa for six months. He would send us snapshots from the big wildlife sanctuaries like Kruger National Park, and on the rare occasion of getting a telephone connection he would tell stories of elephants charging cars and lions approaching to within touching distance. All I wanted to do was go over and join Dad. There was a popular children's TV series called *Daktari* at the time, set in a Nairobi animal orphanage, and I dreamed of joining Clarence the cross-eyed lion and the other animals there.

So it was only natural that after finishing high school I would study to become a vet. At the University of Melbourne, side by side with studying the anatomy and science of animals, my imagination was fired by the British veterinary surgeon David Taylor, who wrote a series of autobiographical books that chronicled his escapades as the 'Zoo Vet'. These books were later adapted for television as the *One to One* series. David Taylor was the first vet to specialise in zoo and wildlife medicine and he worked with zoos, wildlife parks and circuses around the world.

I was captivated by how he worked with his 'patients': an elephant with a toothache, a giant panda with stomach ulcers or an egg-bound emu. He had a flair for improvising new treatments; for example, he treated a haemorrhaging whale by feeding it black puddings, and he fitted a prosthetic beak onto an ailing hornbill.

As a boy, David Taylor had set up a small animal 'hospital' in his family home. As he wrote in his book, at first his parents tolerated the 'toads convalescing in the bathroom cupboard, the paralysed owl that sat on top of the grandfather clock in the hall and the rabbit road accident victims that either regained vitality or wasted away in the emergency wards I established in empty zinc washing tubs'.

Needless to say, I felt David Taylor's books were speaking to me. He did it all with such humour and style. He was my hero and this was when it became very clear to me that I wanted to be not just a vet but a zoo vet.

After graduating I grabbed the first opportunity I could to work with the big animals. My chance came when a part-time job opened up at the Bacchus Marsh Lion Safari Park, not too far from my home in Melbourne. By a happy coincidence there was also a veterinarian in town who needed a young vet for two or three days a week. It meant I could put a full-time job together, working with cats and dogs half the time and indulging my passion for the wild things the rest of the time.

The Bacchus Marsh Lion Safari Park was a phenomenon of its times, enjoying a short but colourful life in the seventies and eighties. Now you'll find it filed under 'Great Theme Parks We Once Had'.

The park was an attempt to cash in on a hunger people had to be amongst the big animals, just like the great wildlife parks of Africa. It was a zoo without the cages. Instead you could drive through large open enclosures and experience the animals close up, from the safety and comfort of your car. It was set up by the old Ashton's Circus, which used the park as a place to keep its circus animals. Ashton's was on the approaches to Melbourne and its great competitor, Bullen's Circus, had a similar set-up on the outskirts of Sydney.

The name is slightly misleading. There weren't only lions but also tigers, buffalos, monkeys and, indeed, camels.

In truth the lion park was a bit of a seat-of-the pants operation and it had its fair share of accidents. What happens if people are busy looking at wildlife as they're driving? They run into the rear of the car in front of them. And what's the first thing they do then? They get out of their car. Then they realise there's a lion next to them. So we had some close calls. Indeed, over the years there were instances of people being bitten and even mauled to death.

Security was a little lax, too, when it came to the animals. There was the time the boys in control of the gates screwed up and let the lions in with the tigers. Eventually we got in with our vehicles and managed to separate them, but the lions had destroyed the tigers and we spent the next week picking up the pieces. In a proper zoo that kind of big cat mayhem just doesn't happen.

Then there was the time two baboons escaped and got up into the top of the observation tower behind the lion enclosure. Baboons are a nasty piece of work at the best of times; one of them had already bitten off the finger of a handler who'd ventured too close during feeding time. They're also super-athletic, and they're smart. These two had occupied the observation room, which was like a guard's room in a watchtower. Once there they kept vigil, opening and closing the door to see who might be trying to get to them. It was impossible to go up the ladder because they had that well covered, so my job was to work my way up the back of the tower and then dart them with a blowpipe through a gap in the timber at the rear of the observation room.

I managed to get a clean hit on the first one, at which point it went absolutely troppo. It started screaming and went bouncing off the walls then reached behind itself and pulled the dart out, though too late to stop the effect of the tranquilliser. Then the other one started going berserk too. It took about five minutes before the first baboon was out cold, and finally the second one calmed down so I was able to get a clean shot on it as well and complete the operation.

Later it was the turn of the Himalayan tahrs, a large beast which is akin to a wild goat. They staged a mass breakout when ten of them jumped the fence in the company of three Barbary sheep and galloped into the Lerderderg Gorge at the rear of the lion park. A tahr won't kill you but it was a definite no-no to have an exotic species like that running amok with native fauna. I was told to keep quiet about it in case the park lost its licence and I spent the next six months up early scouring the bushland in a fruitless, search for the AWOL beasts. I left food out laced with tranquillisers and patrolled the area with my dart gun. But I turned up nothing.

One day a local farmer called to say he had some strange sheep in his paddock and could someone please come and have a look. Sure enough, there were six of the original ten tahrs and a couple of the Barbaries. I managed to dart them from a distance using my gun and bring them back. Who knows? There could be dozens of them out there now.

The great thing about the lion park was that it gave me the chance to put my skills into practice, though in fact university had ill-prepared me for dealing with exotic animals. The university concentrated on farm and domestic creatures such as pigs, horses, cattle, dogs and cats. I wasn't trained to be a zoo vet. Instead I had to learn it on the fly, which wasn't a bad thing.

Some of what we did was decidedly edgy, and there would have been serious problems if the authorities had known what we were up to. But sometimes you've just got to cut through the rules.

I once took a baby tiger home with me for a couple of days, but as far as I was concerned I had no choice. The little thing was critically ill and I needed to watch it every second.

On another occasion I had an eight-month-old lion that could barely walk because of problems with the growth plates in the knee joints of its hind legs. It needed treatment that we could only supply at the vet clinic in town, so I tranquillised it, threw it in the back of the car and brought it into the surgery to confirm the diagnosis with an x-ray. We performed the operation in a suburban vet clinic at the back of the Bacchus Marsh shopping centre, returned it to the car and drove back through town to the lion park. Imagine getting permission for that one from the local authorities.

The lion park didn't have great medical equipment and there wasn't a lot of expertise on hand when it came to some of the trickier procedures, so I was forced to improvise. Once I was called out to help in the case of a mare that was having trouble giving birth. Horses are very explosive animals so I had to first calm her down with a tranquilliser. It turned out that the foal had already died and was lying awkwardly inside the uterus. In such cases you need to get in fast and cut up the foal inside the horse so you can remove it in pieces. The alternative, a caesarean section, would carry a very high risk of contaminating the mother's abdomen, leading to peritonitis and certain death.

The lion park simply didn't have the necessary equipment so I went home, got down a curtain rod, cut it in half and pushed a thin cutting wire through the tube. With this improvised tool I could perform the procedure without the right instruments and still protect the uterus and thus the mare from trauma. It could have gone either way and I regarded it as something of a triumph that I managed to get the foal out, and keep the mare alive.

It was also at the park that I confronted the mysteries of the camel for the first time, though compared with lions, tigers and tahrs, they were far from my first interest. In fact my first experience was something of a disaster.

I was called on to anaesthetise two camels in the field to prepare them for an operation. The lion park had no information at all on the drugs you need to knock out a camel. I called Melbourne zoo, where I had done some work experience as a student, but no-one there had a clue, either. So I improvised with a bizarre combination of drugs, probably more suited to a horse. It got the job done but in the process one camel got pneumonia and the other went ataxic, meaning it suddenly lost control of its movements and couldn't stand. The poor thing was all legs and neck buckling in on itself, and next thing it tumbled down the hill and finished in a heap at the bottom.

And that was probably an appropriate metaphor for my eighteen months at Bacchus Marsh Lion Safari Park: a bit gung-ho, a bit chaotic and lots of the unexpected.

What I did discover was that zoo vets work very hard, don't make a lot of money and many of them end up divorced because of the workload.

But I loved every minute of it.

Two
The hand of fate

I met my wife, Patti, during my final year of vet science at the University of Melbourne, where Patti was studying criminology. The two of us are impulsive, and together we were completely irrational. Wiser heads counselled us to hold on until after I'd completed my degree to get married, but neither of us wanted to wait. I was expected to graduate with honours but in the end it was just a pass, so maybe those cautious souls had a point. But who cares?

I'm not sure who proposed to whom but it happened during a wine-tasting, which was just perfect. By now my dad had thrown off the shackles of his old job as an industrial chemist in Sydney and moved with my mum, Catherine, who was a microbiologist, to run a vineyard in Glenrowan, Victoria, home of Ned Kelly. My sister, Wendy, and brother, Scott, were still living at home with them. Harry Tinson was on his way to becoming the best maker of fortified wines in Australia. Not bad for a bloke who only ever drank beer at home, Reschs Pilsener at that.

Wine and animals are the two Tinson passions and it appears Patti was happy to sign up for both of them.

A year after we married we had our first baby, Katya. All was right with the world, even if it meant I had to ship out the water python, diamond python and carpet python that once occupied Katya's baby room.

The pythons all ended up with my uni mate Greg Parker, who was a kindred spirit when it came to snakes. Greg already had taipans and a death adder. He also kept a falcon in his house, so naturally we were frequent visitors at his place. Greg later went on to found the Ballarat Wildlife Park so he was a true fellow traveller in the world of killer beasts.

It's one of the occupational hazards of being married to a vet that you also marry his or her animal obsession. When Katya was only two we had a close call at Greg's place. We went downstairs under the house to the secret place where Greg kept his collection of pythons. These are amongst the deadliest snakes in the world and they were being kept in the middle of suburbia, so Greg had to keep it low profile. We were quietly checking out Greg's collection when suddenly we came face to face with the crocodile Greg kept in a cage. The croc must have heard us and thought he was about to be fed, because next thing he'd knocked the lid off his cage and was flying towards us, coming up right next to Katya. He wasn't fully grown yet, but he could easily have bitten Katya's head off. She just stood there saying, 'Cocl, cocl,' before I managed to whisk her away.

Patti lived through the craziness of my time as a zoo vet at Bacchus Marsh but, much as she was happy to go along with the baby tiger in our home, the lion in the car, my early mornings on the hunt for the missing tahrs and the white peacock convalescing after being savaged by a tiger, we both knew the fun would have to end sometime.

Reality is a powerful antidote to dreams. In short, exotic animals might be wonderful but they don't put bread on the table. And like most people we knew, we succumbed to the idea that life was about building your business, buying your first home and settling down to raise the kids. It's what we do, right?

■ ■ ▨

We started a new life at Tweed Heads on the far north coast of New South Wales, where I established my first—and only— business as the friendly neighbourhood vet. In so many ways it was the idyllic family set-up. We had the sand and surf at our doorstep and we went about filling the house with kids and animals.

Baby Erica came along, a sister for Katya. We populated the house with three frogs, lovebirds, a German shepherd, cats and, of course, a small collection of snakes.

Here, too, I was lucky. There was a zoo down the road that allowed me to satisfy my craving for the weird and wild.

I had come to believe that as far as animals went, I would never be emotionally involved. If the family dog has been hit by a car or is suffering a terminal disease, it's always tough to break the news to the owners that putting them down is kinder than keeping them alive. As a vet, if your emotions always came to the surface you simply could not operate. But my experience with the chimpanzees of Coolangatta zoo changed my view of my professional self.

The zoo was moving so it was destocking its animals, chimpanzees included. All the animals were screened for diseases and, in the process, two of the chimps, who were brother and sister, had shown up as potentially positive to tuberculosis. I doubted the finding, but it was enough for the Department of Agriculture to order that the chimps be destroyed and they asked me to do it. I argued against the decision because, as far as I was concerned, it was an overreaction. My point was that the alleged TB was in fact a shadow on the lung, which was probably the result of pleurisy. The chimps had been regular little stars with the public and it was highly likely they'd got something as a result of all that human contact. The department dug in and threatened to issue an official order, so ultimately I had no choice.

I had previously managed on a number of occasions to blow dart the chimps with tranquilliser so we could x-ray them. But the more you did it, the harder it became to get a dart onto them. They came to know exactly what was coming. They are so smart. The minute I put the dart to my lips and puffed up my cheeks, they'd leap off in all directions. Once when I looked away for a minute, the male jumped over, grabbed the dart out of my hand and ripped it to shreds. That little episode made the night's television news under the banner 'Chimp Attacks Vet'. Another time he literally grabbed the dart out of my hand, bent it over and threw it back in my face. It was frightening how quick and how strong they were. This game of dodgem went on for three months. And more often than not there was always a crowd around having a good laugh at my expense.

When it came to tranquillising the chimps before euthanasing them, I took to trying to catch them in the early hours of the morning, away from the glare of television cameras or the attention of an audience. Finally, one of them seemed to just give up. I rolled up to dart him one day and, rather than do one of his usual clever moves, he just sat there and looked at me. It was as though he had decided to accept his ultimate fate. It just didn't seem right. This time I managed to dart him and I reckon before I got in to give him the lethal injection he was dead. He just died straightaway.

Euthanasing that chimp was one of the most haunting things I've had to do as a vet. It was like killing a human—but worse. I still remember that look. He looked at me as if to say, 'You bastard.' He just knew. To make matters worse, the post-mortem confirmed what I had been saying: the chimp did not have TB at all. The one good thing to come out of it was that the department decided not to euthanase his sister. But I had taken the life of an animal when it didn't need to happen, and in so doing I had betrayed the animal's trust. It has never left my conscience.

■ ■ ■

It's a cliché that sons measure themselves against their dads, but in my case it is true. By the age of thirty I was haunted by how little adventure there had been in my life, compared to my father's.

I started to feel that I was on a conveyer belt, heading in one direction. While I enjoyed the challenges of private practice, I had never wanted to spend my life working with Mrs Smith's cats and dogs, but that, indeed, was where life had led me. More and more I was wondering: is this as good as it gets?

Dad was born and raised in Harbin, Manchuria, in the north of China on the border with Russia in the 1930s. His father was British, born in Hong Kong, and he married a Russian woman. The family moved to Shanghai where Dad lived the exotic life of an expat kid, moving between the old Chinese neighbourhoods and the British expat compound, which was a slice of upper-class England with its all its privilege and entitlement.

Japan had been at war with China from 1937, and in 1941 the Japanese entered the Shanghai International Settlement where they lived. Dad was only eleven years old when he and the other expat families who hadn't got out ahead of time were placed into a prisoner of war camp. To me, Dad's life seemed like something out of a movie. And indeed it was a movie. Dad had attended school with JG Ballard, whose 1984 novel

Empire of the Sun exactly depicted the life my father lived. The movie version of the same name was released in 1987 when we were living at Tweed Heads.

When the war ended, Dad came out to Sydney from Shanghai as a seventeen-year-old along with his Russian relatives. He managed to get into university and studied chemistry, even though he had never gone to high school because of the war.

Knowing what I know now about the cruelty of life in the POW camp, I am surprised that Dad could be anything approaching normal. But he was. And though he had a million stories to tell, he hardly ever spoke about what he had seen in the POW camp. He told me once that he was walking down Elizabeth Street, Melbourne, and saw a guy coming the other way who he recognised from the camp. They had paused, looked at each other, said a brief hello and kept walking. I guess neither could see the point in revisiting the past. Or perhaps it was just too hard. In his book, JG Ballard summed up the mental scars by saying it took him twenty years to forget before he could start to remember.

Dad never had a bad word to say about the Japanese even though we know some of the most horrendous things happened. The fact that he wouldn't cast judgement on his captors had a big influence on me. I admired him for it. If anything, Dad brought with him that British reserve. He was very proper about things and always had a stiff-upper-lip saying to hand, like 'it doesn't matter what you do, just be the best at it' and 'never perjure your soul for a penny', which was one of his favourites. But one thing Dad never said was 'I love you'. I guess that was typical of his generation.

It sounds stupid, but to me the fact that Dad grew up in China and had all these adventures in a foreign land (that ended up portrayed in a movie) represented the sort of excitement that I was attracted to. In fact, I think I was even a little bit jealous that he had been in a POW camp.

I always thought my father was the smartest person I'd

ever met. At the same time, I also felt that once Dad came to Australia he was constrained by having to do his best for us. I can't imagine how hard it must have been to go from such an exotic existence to landing in postwar Australia in all its blandness. I never had the conversation with him but I'm certain there were other dimensions to himself that he didn't get to explore.

He did the hard yards, slogging it out on a long daily commute in Sydney to get to work and back. Thank goodness late in life he was able to ditch that and become a great wine-maker. But I felt like Dad didn't get to do all the things he wanted to do and I wanted to make sure that didn't happen to me. I wasn't going to wait anymore. I was at a point in my life where I wanted—indeed, needed—to do something outlandish. I felt the call to be not just a little bit involved but completely involved with wild animals.

I didn't know it at the time but the planets were aligning in a way that would change life as I knew it in very dramatic ways.

■ ■ ■

We like to think we can plan our future in neat, unfolding stages. But in the end, life is what comes to us, often unbidden.

The truth is I never went out looking for camels. They came to me.

It was another day of cats and dogs at our Tweed Heads clinic when I got a call out of the blue. The man on the other end of the line wanted six camels castrated.

It's not every day that your average small-town vet gets asked to remove the testicles of a camel. Dogs and cats? Yes. But camels? I was convinced the call was a joke, maybe one of my mates from Sydney having a bit of fun at my expense. After all, who on earth would even own half a dozen huge humped wild beasts in a town like Tweed Heads?

So the first time I brushed him off. But he called back. The second time I put it to him that he was having a lend of me. But then I realised he wasn't. In fact, I couldn't have been more wrong.

My caller was a man called Paddy McHugh. Why he chose to call me, I'll never know. I guess he looked up local vets in the phone book and my name came up. I made the trip to see Paddy at his farm about an hour's drive away.

Paddy was a shade younger than me, in his late twenties. He was a genuine Crocodile Dundee character, down to the bashed-up leather hat and long, bedraggled hair. Paddy was lean and teak strong, his face and body sun-weathered from a life spent in the outback.

I doubt he had ever spent one day in an office or cooped up with textbooks. We were cut from completely different cloth, but Paddy and I clicked immediately. There was something about him that touched a part of me.

It turned out that Paddy just happened to be Australia's number-one camel fanatic. He'd spent half his life working with camels in the wild, and I could see by the way he handled his own stock that he had an intuitive understanding of their nature. He made a living out of organising camel safaris into the outback for city dwellers who were looking for their own 'camel experience', and the farm I went to was where Paddy kept his camels when he wasn't on the road.

Paddy was also a pioneer. In the years before we met, he and another vet had retraced the steps of the explorers Burke and Wills and embarked on a 1500-kilometre trek by camel from the south-east corner of Queensland to the Gulf of Carpentaria at the top of the state. The journey took three months and nearly all of it was through tough country. They made it to the end, though there were many moments when they wondered what the hell they were doing. The original plan was to make the return trip, but it had been way too arduous and they tossed it in once they'd reached the Gulf.

As a teenager Paddy had also spent months at a time on various treks with his older brother Greg and young Indigenous men from the Hermannsburg community in the Northern Territory, bringing horses, donkeys and camels across to north-western New South Wales. It was Paddy's brother, Greg, who had originally 'fallen into the world of camels', as he put it. But Greg had died from leukaemia and Paddy had taken on his mantle.

Paddy knew the qualities of the camel like no-one else. In fact about the only thing he couldn't do with a camel was remove its testicles, which is why I was there with my anaesthetic kit, scalpel and sutures.

While I got to work, Paddy got talking about a big idea I might be interested in. Paddy knew blokes who knew blokes who were looking to stage the biggest ever camel race in Australia's history. A group of Queensland wheeler-dealers was putting together plans to stage the race in 1988, Australia's bicentennial year. They saw the camel as the unsung hero in opening up Australia's north and the event was to be a way of marking that. Calling it the Great Australian Camel Race, it would start at Uluru in Central Australia and finish on the Queensland coast, covering a distance of more than three thousand kilometres and taking around three months. Paddy knew the territory inside out, so of course he would be at the centre of making the race happen.

Listening to what Paddy had to say, I was left in no doubt that the trip would happen and that Paddy and I would be seeing a lot more of each other. In Paddy I believed I had met not so much my soul mate as my alter ego. Paddy had lit the fuse that ignited the person I always wanted to be.

You could hear the clock ticking.

■ ■ ■

Fate might have delivered the camels to my door via Paddy McHugh but fate also had something very dark in store. To be honest, I still have trouble talking about it.

Patti and I had a third baby girl, called Anya, who was born in January of 1986. Life seemed to be going well and we had absolutely no reason to be concerned, however one day I hadn't been at the clinic long before the phone rang. Patti was in deep distress at the other end: Anya was in her cot and had stopped breathing. I raced out the door, got back home and we sped off to the local hospital.

The same day a massive cyclone had hit the Gold Coast, bringing torrential rain that turned roads into rivers and washed away bridges. We managed to fight our way through to Tweed Heads hospital whereupon we were told that Anya's case was so serious she would have to be sent straight away to the Mater Hospital in Brisbane, a good hour and a half away. Anya was rushed into a waiting ambulance and raced up to Brisbane with Patti and I following closely behind in the driving rain on the now treacherous roads.

The specialists at the Mater told us that Anya had suffered an 'unexplained life-threatening event'. It might have been SIDS. We waited with Anya for three long days as she was placed on full life support but the doctors couldn't work out what was wrong. All they could tell us was she was brain dead and that there was only one option. Anya was only nine weeks old.

I remember the moment so vividly even today. I was standing in the corridor when one of the doctors approached and told us that the brain scan on Anya was flat: there was nothing there. The decision was made that Anya would be disconnected from life support. I stood next to Patti and she appeared to be dealing with the news better than me. I was destroyed.

■   ■   ■

We were given the option to hold Anya when she was disconnected. I thought it was right that one of her parents should hold her as she went. I held her when they killed her; technically, it was euthanasia. She died in my arms and it was the worst thing that has ever happened in my life. I felt like my heart had fallen out. I could have died at that moment.

In a way we had been through this before. Our first daughter, Katya, had narrowly survived an 'unexplained' life-threatening event at the age of eighteen months. Again I was at the clinic when Patti called me in distress. I raced home to find that Katya had been fitting uncontrollably. We bundled her into the car and I spent the longest fifteen minutes of my life with my finger in Katya's mouth, clearing her airways so she could breathe. She was biting so hard she just about chewed my thumb off as we made a dash to the hospital.

Katya managed to survive the 'unexplained life-threatening event'. The doctors theorised that it might have been epilepsy. But it was a terrifying moment, and not least because we didn't know why a perfectly healthy little girl would suddenly lurch so close to death.

But with Anya it was too late. There was no bringing her back. She was gone.

And at that moment I thought I would never let anything hurt me that much again. I have no doubt it has made me who I am today. There is always a part of me that I hold back.

Three
Augathella to Arabia

My answer to the horror of Anya's death was to make myself frantically busy. More and more I was dividing my time between the vet clinic and being out with Paddy McHugh and the camels. And the more time I spent with Paddy, the more respect I developed for this animal. I had caught the bug from Paddy and, to use his phrase, I was falling in with the camels.

Having little or no scientific education in camels, I was coming to understand what made them such fantastic creatures. They were utterly indestructible, capable of surviving the extremes of life in the Australian desert without breaking down. They hardly ever suffered illnesses like other animals do. I learned that if you were stuck in the harshest conditions you could depend on a camel to get you out and keep you safe. I began to feel a connection to camels that I hadn't experienced with any other animal I'd worked with.

There was also what the camel represented. The camel was the spirit of the wild and it could transport you to the pure, simple beauty you find in an empty land. With a camel you could ride out and lose yourself in the isolation of the outback.

At the same time I was becoming more and more involved with Paddy in bringing together the various strands of the Great Australian Camel Race. Paddy suggested that I might like to act as the vet for the camels he was entering in the race, but instead I sold him on the idea that I should be the vet responsible for the entire race.

There was a huge amount of planning to be done to make sure the race could be run safely. Leaving the operation of the vet practice to a trusted locum I would take off for days at a time into Central Australia to help catch camels and gather preliminary data on how camels performed over long distances.

My life was drifting away from the clinic at Tweed Heads. All I could see was a huge adventure in front of me as the official vet for the camel race and I wanted to be part of it. Inevitably that would mean major upheavals. For one thing, I would have to abandon the vet practice for three months and trust that our locum would keep it ticking over. There was also the question of Patti and the girls. Katya was now ten and Erica was six, so there was school to think about.

In the end it was no issue at all. Patti and I decided it would do us a power of good to get away from our surrounds and spend time together on a once in a lifetime adventure. As a family we hadn't recovered from Anya's sudden death, at home, in her cot—a place she should have been safest. How does that happen? We had coped by putting one foot in front of the other and making out to the rest of the world that we were fine, thanks. At the same time, Patti was pregnant again, a form of proof, if you wanted to look at it that way, that we were moving on.

So we packed up the house, took the kids out of school and set off for the centre of Australia for three months. We saw the Great Australian Camel Race as a chance to have a break and renew ourselves. We didn't realise that it would mark the start of a whole new life out of the ashes of the old.

■ ■ ■

The Great Australian Camel Race was a genuine one-off gathering of rogues and big characters.

The idea had originally come from a colourful Queensland businessman called Arthur Earle, one of the infamous 'white shoe brigade' who had made a fortune out of land deals and property development in the time of the then premier, Joh Bjelke-Petersen. Arthur was good friends with Joh, and had organised for him to be the official race starter. Arthur had also organised for prize money of $100,000, a huge amount at the time and aimed at luring the best riders from Australia and all over the world.

On the operations side, the technical mastermind was a former British SAS commander called Noel Dudgeon. Noel had a wealth of experience organising the complex logistics behind military ops. Then in his late sixties, he had planned the race meticulously.

The Australian Army was also heavily involved on the operational side. A unit from Brisbane would be deployed to feed the support staff, and to act as timekeepers and tail-end Charlies at the back of the race providing communications to those at the front.

In fact the race would be as much a PR exercise for the military as anything else. We had commandoes, guys from the 2nd/4th Battalion of the Royal Australian Regiment from Townsville, and the Special Air Service Regiment from Swanbourne in Perth. It was a huge military presence and the race could not have happened without it.

Above all, Arthur Earle, Paddy McHugh and the rest of us wanted this to be a showcase for the camels. Most Australians have no idea how important camels have been to opening up the north of the country. The camel has enormous strength and endurance; it can carry close to a tonne of weight, far more than a horse or bullock can. Camel drays pull telegraph poles and railway sleepers. And the camel never failed—whatever it was supposed to do, it did, and it never broke down.

The race would be a serious test of endurance over some of the most difficult terrain imaginable: 3300 kilometres, starting from Uluru and tracking across the Northern Territory and Queensland before finishing on the Gold Coast. We had broken the route down into a series of legs, like a car rally, with checkpoints along the way so each competitor could be timed. We had put together what was in effect a military campaign, with our 'army' of competitors and camels taking on the enemy of a hostile environment. As the days ticked down to the start of the Great Australian Camel Race every move was checked and double-checked. Every possible contingency was catered for.

Or so we thought.

■   ■   ■

The sixty-nine camels and riders plus support teams, race officials and military guys gathered for the start just before sunrise on 23 April 1988.

For the competitors this was serious business, but there was also a festive air to the occasion, with wives, children, dogs and even the odd long-distance runner blow-in who had decided to join the pack. There was also a documentary crew along, recording what was meant to be a great romantic adventure: man and beast pitted against the elements.

Just after sunrise, Joh Bjelke-Petersen fired the starting gun for the first leg from Uluru to Alice Springs, a relatively easy 416 kilometres.

As race vet I had enormous responsibilities. It was my job to make sure the camels were in good enough physical shape to withstand the rigours of the race. I carried with me a blood chemistry machine so I could do ongoing blood testing and check on how quickly the camels' hearts recovered from each day's exertions.

It was very clear within forty-eight hours that the camels weren't going to be the problem. We had allowed three days to complete the first leg, but some of the camels managed to get there in half that time. It was a promising beginning.

All was proceeding smoothly when, five days into the race, our former SAS commander Noel Dudgeon collapsed with kidney disease and was forced to retire. Suddenly I found myself thrust into the role of race director. This meant I was now responsible not just for the animals but the humans as well, and very soon I was to be confronted with a genuine crisis. Months of meticulous planning were about to unravel. Spectacularly.

We had staged the race from late April because that's when the climate is normally at its best, with pleasant temperatures no higher than about twenty-seven degrees Celsius in the day and lows of around twelve degrees at night. It also took us outside the tropical rainy season, so we could expect the odd shower but nothing like the downpours you get in January, February and March.

This year, though, the rain had bucketed down so torrentially just prior to the beginning of the race that the sewage pits at Alice Springs caravan park had overflowed and flooded the grounds. When we arrived there to set up camp at the end of our first leg, the grounds were nice and dry. But, unbeknownst to us, the rains had left a nasty legacy: a bacteria called *Shigella dysenteriae*, which is every bit as bad as it sounds.

After breaking camp in Alice Springs we headed off for the town of Boulia, over seven hundred kilometres away and taking us from the Northern Territory into Queensland. This was to be one of the longest and most arduous legs of the race. A couple of days out of Alice Springs as we headed for the top of the Simpson Desert, disaster hit.

People started dropping with a severe case of gastro. One of the first was my daughter, Erica, who was only six. The onslaught was so bad that she was literally passing the lining of her bowel. Having already lost Anya, we were terrified about the prospects for our little girl. Taking no chances, Patti and I got Erica into a car and drove her back to Alice Springs Base Hospital where she was kept for forty-eight hours. Luckily she bounced back but tests revealed that she had suffered a severe bout of dysentery. Putting two and two together, we could trace it back to the Alice Springs caravan park.

Erica rejoined us but the further we pressed on, the more people were getting hammered with this horrendous dysentery. Suddenly the great romantic adventure had turned into a full-blown public health crisis, with the real prospect that people might die. And I was in charge.

We still had a hundred or so kilometres to go to reach Boulia. The military guys had pitched camp in a dry section of the Georgina River on Glenormiston Station, just over the Queensland border, and meanwhile the rain had started to bucket down to the north of us. I knew there was a wall of water heading our way. I told them that if they didn't get out then they were going to get washed away. But the military, of course, listens only to itself and by the time they got themselves organised it was too late. Before long, heavy-duty army trucks were bogged in wheel-deep mud and just couldn't move. So we were not only desperately ill, we were also bogged. And at that stage we started losing track of where everyone had got to. Some were so sick they were literally hunched over with diarrhoea as their mates positioned themselves behind them, shovelling away the mud and excrement in the driving rain. The scenes were like a bad third world refugee camp.

We attempted to push on through the rains, but the camels too were finding it heavy going, with some of them getting stuck in mud and water up to their chests. We had to lasso them with straps around their belly or their rear and drag them out. Sixteen-wheeler military semitrailers were bogged and had to be pulled out by trucks. As I attempted to move from one crisis to the next, I found the lights of my four-wheel drive were at times literally under water.

Things were spinning out of control. We were marooned in the middle of nowhere, it felt like everyone around me was dying, and we were still a long way from decent medical help.

There was no choice but to suspend the race. I told everyone we had to get to Boulia as fast as possible. I didn't care how they did it—they could carry the camels as far as I was concerned. We just had to sort this out.

We finally limped into the town and started to get a grip on the deteriorating situation. There was panic, anger, disappointment, despair: every emotion you could imagine. In the midst of this I called a meeting at the community hall of all 160 people on the race, who we divided into three groups: those affected by the disease and still had it, those who'd been affected and had recovered, and those who hadn't yet been affected.

The Royal Flying Doctor Service ferried some of the worst cases to regional hospitals, including our race leader who spent three days on a drip at Mount Isa Base Hospital after his kidneys shut down. We all thought he was a sure bet to win the whole race. Next thing we feared he would be the first to die. We got every antibiotic we could find within a thousand kilometres of us and had them brought to the Boulia community hall, which acted as medical HQ. The Royal Flying Doctor Service also treated those who couldn't be flown out. Dozens of the sick were camped out in tents at the local racetrack, which took on the appearance of a makeshift hospital ward.

You could hear the moans and groans as you walked through the tent hospital. Some were literally at death's door. We were meant to be raising money for the Royal Flying Doctor, so it wasn't lost on me that we might be costing them more than they would get.

Meanwhile, a small group who weren't sick had decided to head out on a day trip to a nearby town named Urandangie. We later heard that they unwittingly spread the disease there, too. So we had introduced what became known as the 'camel plague' across Queensland and our race had become notorious, in Australia and around the world.

The reality of what happened—and the publicity—might have been bad, but ultimately we got those people back on their feet and moving across the country, with no fatalities and no camels dying either. God knows how we did it, but it will always be my greatest achievement. There had been two record rains in the middle of the desert when it should have been dry. It was absolutely horrendous. It's a miracle that no-one died by drowning, by *Shigella* or by simply disappearing.

Just about everybody ended up sick except for me. I got by on three to four hours' sleep for weeks on end. Maybe it was the adrenalin that got me through, but it felt as though I was on a mission to get these people out safe and sound. With the help of our military support and the Royal Flying Doctor Service we did it. The experience made me feel I was bulletproof.

The Great Australian Camel Race moved on after its brush with disaster, but tensions between the military men and the civilians simmered just below the surface. There was one major blow-up when a former SAS military commander turned on the bloke who'd supplied him with what he considered to be a dud camel. This led to blows and I was forced to take the matter to the Queensland constabulary, where the case oddly enough went no further.

The race itself didn't get the headlines we were hoping for, but those who took part learned a thing or two about the remarkable resilience of these animals. What other beast could transport human beings over 3000 kilometres of sand, dust, mud, heat and torrential rain?

In the end only twenty-four of the sixty-nine starters managed to complete every leg of the race. The camels were fine: it was only ever the humans who couldn't carry on. I got some idea of how tough it was when I did a three-day ride, which turned into a full-on battle with my camel, who wanted to be rid of me. My rear end was just about destroyed and I had trouble walking for days.

But I was just blown away with what the camels achieved. Not only did they cover distances no-one believed possible but they did it at an incredible pace. On one of the legs a camel travelled 220 kilometres in twenty-three hours, an average of about ten kilometres an hour and done without rest.

As a vet it was an eye-opening experience to see the camel not only do what you wanted it to but also do just about everything better than other animals. That's when my fascination for the camel really grew exponentially, along with my respect.

■ ■ ■

There was to be one final twist in the tale of the Great Australian Camel Race.

We had just about reached the three-quarter mark and were bunked down in a town called Augathella, near Charleville. I was having a beer at the local pub when a car pulled up outside. A man stepped out, introduced himself to me and asked if I might have time to talk. My unexpected visitor explained that he represented the royal family of Abu Dhabi and that he had been sent by 'someone very important'. His mission was to find me and offer me a job to set up a hospital for camels in the United Arab Emirates.

The man bearing the offer was Heath Harris. Heath is one of those larger than life characters and a man with a natural—and valuable—instinct for working with animals; amongst other achievements he had trained the horses for the classic Australian feature films, *Breaker Morant, Gallipoli* and *The Man from Snowy River*. Already a legend amongst Australian horse trainers, for now he was working for the ruling family of the oil-rich Gulf emirate of Abu Dhabi, where he was in charge of improving their racehorse stock. Now they wished to have someone do for their camels what Heath had done for their horses.

I was, of course, flattered and not quite sure what to say. Standing in the Augathella pub it all seemed so improbable, but Heath was clearly deadly serious. In fact he had been trying to track me down for a good month and at one stage had even hired a small plane to land along our route through the Northern Territory. It turned out that every time he tried to land he was stopped by a local cockie parking his truck on the airstrip. It was no mystery to us why: we'd been copping a lot of criticism from the animal lib people, especially after an incident when some of the camels had been mired in mud. We were convinced that any plane trying to land was carrying animal rights activists wanting to stop the race. And, given their sympathies, it wasn't too hard to get the local cockies to lend a hand.

This had apparently gone on for weeks. Poor Heath had started on his mission to get me when we were crossing over the top of the Simpson Desert, just after our ill-fated stay in Alice Springs. He'd returned twice to Sydney and eventually decided the only solution was to get in front of the race, hire a four-wheel drive and then drive back down the road.

Heath summed up the whole schmozzle succinctly: 'Fuck, mate, all I wanted to do was offer you a job!'

When the Abu Dhabi royal family had asked Heath to work on their camels, he had replied, as only Heath can, 'Yes, of course. I'll get you the best camel vet in the world.'

It wasn't the first—or the last— time that Heath would gild the lily and then paddle fast to make good on his promises later. I felt that my experience, at the age of thirty-three—having anaesthetised two camels, castrated six of them and been in charge of an endurance race—left me a long way short of Heath's 'best in world' boast, though in truth there probably wasn't a lot of competition in the west.

Heath jokes that all he had to do was offer me a hot shower in the Augathella hotel and a half-decent meal, such was the state I was in after close to two months on the road. He was pretty right. But I was also ready to move on. The last thing I wanted to do after the adrenalin charge of the Great Australian Camel Race was return to my old life in a Tweed Heads vet surgery.

As far as I was concerned, there was no doubt. Nevertheless, it was a big decision.

Heath was looking to build a team of three vets. He already had one Australian vet on board who, though highly experienced, was not a camel expert. So, apart from myself as the camel specialist, he was looking for one more. I rang my business partner in the surgery, Doug Cluer, and put it to him: 'What do you say we up stumps and head to the Middle East?' It wasn't easy for Doug. His wife was a doctor and they, too, had young kids to think about.

For my part, I had never been out of Australia; Kangaroo Island had been my only 'overseas' trip. I also had a race to finish. On top of that, Patti was now six months pregnant and was due a month or so after the race finished. So we would have to contend with a massive upheaval for the whole family at the precise time Patti was due to give birth. But, as always, Patti was up for the adventure.

It didn't take us long to make the decision. We agreed in principle and Heath went back to the potential employer he was dealing with—who that was exactly we couldn't know, because Heath wasn't allowed to tell us.

Meanwhile, I set about trying to gather some information on where I might be spending the next chunk of my life. My geography is not bad and while I'd heard of Dubai, I'd never heard of Abu Dhabi, which is in fact the capital of the United Arab Emirates. I knew where Bahrain was. As a kid I'd collected stamps from Sharjah, though I had no concept of exactly where it was. And I also had stamps from Muscat and Oman from the old days when they were two different places. But basically it was all a big mystery.

One day I took Patti and the kids up to the library to research the United Arab Emirates and, more importantly, the town of Al Ain, where we would be living. Even though it is the hometown of Abu Dhabi's royal family, there wasn't a lot of information on Al Ain, which is located in the desert about a hundred kilometres inland, and a mere dot on the border with Oman. We imagined we might be living in a tent in the middle of nowhere.

I learned we were bound for a nation that had existed for only sixteen years, was governed by an all-powerful family and had Islam as its religion—at which point I remember thinking, 'Well, no alcohol.'

Official portraits of the UAE's ruler showed a weathered and stern face that spoke of a man who would brook no dissent. It seemed to me that this place was not just on the other side of the world but perhaps from another world altogether.

But a man had travelled from across the Middle East to pluck me out of the backblocks of Australia. It was as though I was being pulled by destiny.

Doug and I decided to lease the business out to another vet, head over to the UAE and just see what happened. Maybe we'd be back; maybe we wouldn't.

Under the terms of the contract we had to do three months' probation without our families. I stayed in Australia for the birth of our baby girl, Natalia, on the eighth day of the eighth month in 1988. Could there be a better birthdate for a bicentennial baby? A couple of weeks later I waved goodbye to Patti, Katya, Erica and our newborn and jumped on a plane with Doug and Heath.

■ ■ ■

It was Barry Humphries who once said that living in Australia your entire life was like going to a party and staying in the kitchen all night. But what would the party be like in the UAE? I had not the faintest idea. I was truly flying into the unknown. Having never set foot outside of Australia, I didn't even own a suitcase.

Now I was on my first trip and flying business class, courtesy of the oil sheikhs of the Middle East. The salary was substantial. There were performance bonuses on offer. The kids' school fees would be paid for. Accommodation was supplied. And it was all tax-free. What's not to like about that?

These were (and largely still are) the standard conditions for a senior westerner being employed in the Gulf. It was a system that began in the sixties to compensate western experts for stepping off their career ladder and upping sticks from the comforts of London or Sydney to the barely developed and intolerably hot desert climate of the UAE, where temperatures commonly reach fifty degrees Celsius in summer. It was hardship money, and it was necessary to lure the best people to a country that badly needed all the expertise it could get to build a modern functioning state from scratch.

Up until just before our flight I still did not know who I was working for, but by the time the boarding passes were issued we discovered who we would be answering to. It was the Crown

Prince of Abu Dhabi, first son of the Ruler of Abu Dhabi, the wealthiest, most powerful emirate of the UAE.

Heath Harris had already spent some months in the employ of the UAE royal family and was by now accustomed to the benefits that can confer on you. He was able to fill in some of the missing pieces about the whys and wherefores of the project we'd be working on.

Heath had met a well-connected UAE local called Abdullah al Baadi while in Russia where Heath was buying thoroughbreds for a wealthy Australian businessman and Abdullah was buying for the Abu Dhabi ruling family. Abdullah invited Heath to the Middle East to work his magic with the royal family's horses. Somewhere along the line Heath ended up at a camel camp and, in his inimitable fashion, started messing around with one of the camels. I've never seen anyone like him for training animals, and it seems that he did a few tricks on this camel and soon had it doing exactly what the locals wanted. It was then that Abdullah got an idea: he wanted Heath to start a new camel hospital—which is where I came in. Sitting on the plane, I still had no real idea what it would mean to work for the Crown Prince; I guessed it might be something like working for the Queen of England. As to what went on in the Middle East, well, I had seen the movie *The Black Stallion*, which was set in North Africa featuring a sheikh. And, of course, there was *Lawrence of Arabia*, one of my favourite films. So it was Peter O'Toole and Alec Guinness playing an Arabian prince who had given me my best—and indeed only—impression of where I was going. But as I was to learn, *Lawrence of Arabia* is about as useful a guide to Arabia as *The Man from Snowy River* is to Australia. It might have been an Oscar-winning movie but in the end it was little more than a collection of colonial-era stereotypes that bore no relation at all to the reality of Bedouin life.

Alone with my thoughts as we hurtled through the night, I reflected on how fate and chance meetings had brought me into the world of the camels. I was ready to live a life without borders.

Four
A work in progress

Welcome to Arabia.

The door from business class opened to a blast of hot Arabian Gulf air, a special concoction that comes mixed with the smell of avgas and bitumen. It was early in the morning and still pitch black. There to greet us was Heath's man, Abdullah al Baadi, the architect of our future. Clad in flowing white robes, Abdullah was accompanied by a blue-uniformed security official carrying a massive machine gun. We were escorted down the steps of the plane to a room inside the terminal reserved for VIPs. All golden chandeliers and gold-embossed single-seater chairs, it was an area normally set aside for receiving the sheikhs of other Gulf countries.

A waiter brought Arabic coffee, dispensed from a golden pot into fine golden cups. While others were queuing to go through the elaborate process of being issued a work visa, our passports were quickly taken, stamped and returned to us before we were escorted into the back of a black Mercedes 500.

We were introduced to our own driver, Hamza, who would become our private chauffeur during our stay. On this occasion Hamza took our luggage and went ahead while Heath, Doug and I travelled with Abdullah in the Merc to our hotel in Abu Dhabi. Abdullah thoughtfully handed me a mobile phone to call my wife and tell her I had arrived safe and sound.

So this was what happened when you worked for the Crown Prince: an armed escort and no need to mill with the masses in immigration. It was my first taste of the kudos that surrounds the son of the ruler of the UAE. I found it hard to get my head around the special privilege that comes not just from having power but also from working for someone who has that power.

The next day we were summoned to a grand villa set in extensive grounds for a welcome lunch with twenty of Abu Dhabi's leading Emiratis, all friends of our sponsor, Abdullah al Baadi.

We took our seats at a table replete with the finest food of the Arab world, as well as local specialties like roasted goat on a bed of rice and garnished with sultanas and pine nuts. So far, this was all in keeping with the Arab Gulf stereotypes I had managed to acquire: the idea of the grand welcome to the stranger, all orchestrated by a glowering subaltern with a clap of the hands and a snap of the fingers.

The room was alive with the sounds of Arabic, and our hosts kindly made us welcome by also speaking in English. Chatting away politely, I had just started to feel comfortable in this exotic setting when, out of the corner of my eye, I could see something quite extraordinary taking place. In strode another Abu Dhabi business figure in customary white robes—with a mountain lion on a leash.

There were laughs and hurrahs, a hubbub of Arabic calls and exclamations. What fun. What entertainment. And no-one was in the least perturbed to have this wild cat in the room, an incredibly muscular and athletic animal that kills its prey by leaping at the neck, breaking it and then feasting.

I exchanged a 'what the fuck' glance with Doug Cluer. Here we were, good Australian boys fresh from the Gold Coast, accustomed to rules for this and rules for that, suddenly blown away. Our elegant but deadly companion stayed lashed to a pole but still within metres of us as we attempted to resume our polite conversation. Within forty-eight hours of arriving I had stepped inside the private world of the Emiratis and witnessed one of those moments that ninety-nine per cent of foreigners never get to see. Money can buy a lot of things, it seems, even a wild cat imported—heaven knows how—from the United States.

When I saw that wild mountain lion being casually led in, as if it was a pet labrador, it made me think that these are my kind of people—and this is my kind of place.

■ ■ ■

After three days of twiddling our thumbs in Abu Dhabi and wondering what might happen next, we were summoned to move out. Speeding along a strip of newly cut highway through near empty desert, air-conditioned against the heat in a BMW saloon, we made for our new home in the interior of the country. A vast unpopulated landscape stretched before us, with sand out to the horizon.

As we approached from the flat of the desert, the landscape softened to something more welcoming. Here was the sprawl-ing oasis town of Al Ain, rising unexpectedly out of barren surrounds. There were date palms. There was grass. There were beds of flowers on the side of the road, at the roundabouts and on the median strip. Al Ain is a small dot in the corner of the UAE and not far from the Empty Quarter, the largest expanse of desert in the world. For the Bedouin this oasis was a lifesaver, a place where you arrived after days of travelling across the desert to find a reliable supply of water. It was as if, by magic, a garden had sprung up in the desert.

We were in the rural heart of the UAE, in a regional town with a population numbering around 100,000, nearly all of them Bedouin, with only a few hundred western expats. I arrived to find that my home on the outer edges of Al Ain was nothing more than an idea sketched in the sand, itself surrounded by a sea of endless sand. The third member of our vet team, Geoff Manefield, had already been on the job for a month or so. Geoff was an amateur architect and had drawn up plans for a large residence with four bedrooms, including a room for a maid, and four separate bathrooms, a pointer to the grander lifestyle we would be enjoying as a family. But it would be at least three months before it was built, hopefully just in time for Patti and our three girls to arrive.

In the meantime, I would be holed up in one of only two hotels that catered to westerners, the Hilton. Al Ain was hardly a tourist destination, so the hotel served as a home away from home for foreigners such as oil company executives and defence contractors who were visiting on business and typically working at locations out in the desert.

And that's where we were greeted by our immediate boss, Mr Zuhair. Indeed, the Hilton was Mr Zuhair's second home. He would take his regular seat in the hotel café every evening to drink coffee with whoever happened by and to generally hold court.

We might have looked good on paper, and Heath might have vouched for us, but in the end, if Mr Zuhair didn't think we were right for the job, all bets were off. Mr Zuhair ran the local date factory on behalf of the Crown Prince, Sheikh Khalifa. In an earlier life he had been the Crown Prince's teacher and had now become his confidante and agricultural adviser. He therefore had a direct line to the sheikh and his judgements could ultimately make or break us.

In the way of Arab businessmen, Mr Zuhair was superb at relationships. He would frequently talk about anything but business while at the same time making rapid assessments on your qualities as a human. Could you be trusted or not? Were you hiding something? Or were you who you said you were? The Emiratis had lost their innocence when it came to foreigners who washed up in the UAE, attracted to the promise of riches, like bees to a honey pot. If you were a charlatan or a spiv, Mr Zuhair would find you out before you did too much damage.

Mr Zuhair beckoned us to sit and take coffee with him. He wanted to expand on the Crown Prince's vision and explain the personal dimension of the task. Abu Dhabi was by far the largest of the seven emirates of the UAE. It held ninety per cent of the country's oil, so it was also by far the wealthiest emirate. The Ruler of Abu Dhabi, Sheikh Zayed, had driven the unification of the seven emirates and was the founding president of the UAE. Abu Dhabi was the capital, but Al Ain was special because it was the ancestral home of Sheikh Zayed and his son, the Crown Prince. They were from the Al Nahyan family, which had ruled Al Ain and its surrounds for centuries. Yet for all this pedigree, when it came to the camel races, Abu Dhabi was not even in the hunt. In the Gulf pecking order, the Crown Prince's camels ranked number six, pretty well dead last.

Power was one thing. Camels were quite another. Both the president and the Crown Prince were real camel men. The president had his own racing camel stock, as did some of the other less powerful sheikhs in the Emirate. But the Crown Prince wanted Abu Dhabi to use the best of international practice and western science: His Highness wanted no less than the best veterinary and training facility for camels in the world. He wanted to revolutionise camel racing in the Gulf and he was happy to back the project, whatever the cost.

The mission was clear. We had to get the Crown Prince's camels to the point where Abu Dhabi could beat Dubai or

Qatar or Kuwait or any other Gulf State. The cash prizes were great, but money was largely irrelevant for the wealthiest of men. This was all about the pride of tribal leaders and the prestige of Abu Dhabi. And that meant winning the ultimate racing prize, the Golden Sword.

Now it was up to us to make it happen. In addition to our homes, Geoff had sketched out plans for a clinic with offices and blood analysis labs. But, apart from that, there was nothing. It was our job to work out a blueprint for the facilities, supervise construction and get the right equipment.

There were legions of foreign expats in the UAE, hired on short-term contracts to build hospitals, schools, universities, airports, highways, desalination plants, water systems and so on: all the essentials to make a functioning modern society in a land that only twenty or so years before hadn't even had reliable electricity.

But our task was something different. Camels were personal. They were integral to tribal history. Along with the falcon, which the Emiratis traditionally used for hunting, for centuries the camel had been essential for survival in the desert. They were used to wage war, gather food, and carry families from settlement to settlement. Camels were the heart and soul of what it meant to be an Emirati.

To say I felt underqualified would be an understatement. Yet I would be directing the future of the camel for the tribal heads of these lands.

I had no idea how long I would be here. For all I knew, I might be judged not up to the task and tossed aside in weeks or months. Luckily, Mr Zuhair was an excellent organiser, spoke good English and was well disposed to Australians. He'd visited Australia many times and was a man of immense goodwill. He wanted us to succeed. But at the same time, he needed this project to work for the sake of his relationship with the Crown Prince. We might be judged on our performance, but he would be judged on his judgements.

'Convince me about your plans and we will back you,' he said. 'First I want you to see how our camels race and then get back to me. Hamza will pick you up in the morning. Five o'clock.'

It was like starting with a blank canvas and the effect was quite liberating.

■   ■   ■

Hamza duly presented himself before dawn for the drive out to the racetrack at a small backblock town called Al Wathba, about an hour away.

The drive took us back along the main road to Abu Dhabi before branching off down a narrow, isolated road. We were tracking away from the new UAE, into areas almost untouched by development.

As the morning sun rose, it cast a pale light across the still sands of the desert, no sign yet of the heat of the day. Looking out from the back of the car I caught my first sight of the Arabian camel in its natural habitat. They emerged in the distance, in groups of two and three, drifting serenely across the sands. With a slow, elegant gait, they set the pace of life in the desert. This is where they belonged and this was their domain. It lent them an air of arrogance, a sense that they had total control in a place too tough for others to survive. There could be nothing that would hurry a camel. It was at peace with these surroundings.

In the silence of the early morning it was easy to feel the eternal quality of the desert. It has existed forever and will exist forever after you and I are gone. There was beauty in the nothingness of the endless sand, yet there was menace at the same time. Here a camel is your friend, your companion, your saviour. Without it you would die.

For kilometre after kilometre there was nothing more than flat desert and small clusters of camels. It was easy to imagine that this was how the Bedouin had lived for centuries before the discovery of oil: a land without borders, where you survived in an unforgiving climate.

The Al Wathba races were mainly for the local Bedouin tribes, but word today was that the Crown Prince's camels would also be running.

We were the first to arrive at the track. It was similar to going to Australian country horse races with one huge difference. A horse track will normally be about three kilometres long at most but camels race much greater distances. In the not too distant past, camels had galloped across a flat, straight track off into the distance, for up to ten kilometres.

That was changing. Al Wathba was one of the first circular tracks, which meant the race would start and end at the same point. It also meant an enormous track that stretched far out, before turning back for home.

Like the rest of the country, the Al Wathba complex was a work in progress. A track of compacted dust and sand had been prepared, but there was no grandstand. Instead there was a flat area with an enormous tent about fifty metres from the track, on a slightly raised piece of land. Inside the tent about a hundred chairs were set out in rows. The twenty or so at the front and centre were of the ornate, gilt-edged, high-backed variety, complete with golden tassels, similar to those I had sat in at the airport. This was confirmation that VIPs would be attending.

I was given few clues as to what to expect, but something told me I shouldn't sit in the very front row in case somebody more important than me should come along. So I plonked myself down in the middle of the second row.

Meanwhile, the first of the Bedouin turned up, in a weather-beaten Toyota ute with a camel squatting in the rear, which I soon discovered was pretty typical. Others arrived walking their animals on a long leather lead. These were the men of the desert: lean and sinewy, hardened against the sun and toughened by a centuries-long fight for survival. Some greeted each other by shaking hands. Most greeted each other by rubbing noses, in the way of tradition. They were bursting with life.

There was a minor stir as the first of the official entourages arrived. This was a local sheikh, the head of a minor tribe and probably ten or more rungs down the pecking order, but still a man to be honoured by those beneath him. There was more commotion as other sheikhs arrived, each one higher up the pecking order than the one before. As each sheikh arrived, he was instantly surrounded by local Bedouin competing to show their respect. Eventually all the sheikhs were seated and their cars driven away by hangers-on.

By now two hours had passed. For a while nothing at all happened and I kept thinking, okay, that's it, the race will start now. The tent was full. The camels were milling around down below at the side of the tent; there was the occasional roar or grunt or spit. And yet nothing was happening.

And then in the distance there appeared a massive cloud of dust, ten times bigger than anything else before it. As it drew nearer I could make out half a dozen Toyota pickups with machine guns on the back, held by men dressed in blue-grey uniforms. Out jumped bodyguards wearing long white robes clutching Kalashnikovs, with machine-gun bullet belts strung diagonally across their chests. And behind the first ten or so cars was a massive Pullman stretch limousine. This was the President of the United Arab Emirates, Sheikh Zayed bin Sultan Al Nahyan.

Upon his arrival, all the sheikhs rose as one and bustled over to make their greetings. The excitement was enormous. Hundreds of Bedouin pressed around the man they revered as the 'great sheikh'; everyone wanted a piece of him, to touch him, to have him acknowledge them. The sheikh moved deliberately through the throng. Followers approached and bent their heads to kiss the sleeve of his right arm. In the end there was a melee of sheikhs and Bedouin crowded around this one man. It was the most powerful expression of pure adulation I had ever seen for one human being.

Not knowing what to do, I stayed in my seat and looked on. I was the only westerner there. And I felt like it.

When the president entered the official tent he took his seat in the middle of the front row. The face I saw here was very different to the stern visage that stared out at me from the pages of the encyclopaedia I'd consulted before leaving Australia. It was a face of calm authority that would readily break out into a wide smile and a laugh at the sight of a close friend. At the age of seventy or more, his body remained wiry and strong. Above all this was a man who radiated charisma and commanded not just the respect of his people but their love. It was a relationship the like of which I had never seen.

For all the affection, though, he was still a head of state, and security was heavy. With the president sitting pretty much right in front of me, I ended up spending the morning with his guards next to me and the barrel of a Kalashnikov shoved up my left nostril.

I had come to watch a camel race, but what I got was an instant education in how the UAE really works.

This was a tribal society where hierarchy was everything. But at the same time, there was nothing remote about the ruler. With a population which ran only into the hundreds of thousands, it was possible for Sheikh Zayed to know everyone by name, to know their families, who had been born, who had died, who was ill, who needed help, who had excelled, who was lagging behind. It was an intensely personal way to govern a country.

This is what a desert society produces. You respect your leader, your leader protects you. Without your leader you are nothing. Your leader dispenses favours and works to defend your interests.

The desert strips you back to the basics of survival. You make alliances. You help each other. You live together or you die apart. You protect what you have. You help strangers who arrive on your doorstep. You give your visitor the last rice on your plate. And you repel danger with a gun.

Hierarchy extended to time as well. The leader must never be kept waiting for anyone. The least important must arrive early and wait, which perhaps explains why I was the first to be brought to the racetrack that day. And herein lay an important clue for my future: no matter how important I might think I was or how valued my skills were, the welfare of the locals always came first.

The races were almost an anticlimax after the frenzy triggered by the arrival of the president.

The camels lined up fifteen or twenty across, with no barrier or starting gate to hold them. At that time, the jockeys were very young boys, aged about eight to eleven, typically from Bangladesh. At the starting shout, the camels heaved off, kicking up a storm of sand and dust. Before long they were so far off into the distance that it was all but impossible from our tent to get any sense of who was in the lead. A full fifteen minutes later the group returned into view to round the final bend and head for the finishing line.

It might not have been the greatest spectacle and it was only a relatively minor event as far as race meetings go, but even here the prizes were substantial. The winner of every race received a new four-wheel drive, such as a Landcruiser. There were cash prizes all the way down to tenth place, all gifted by the local sheikhs.

Apart from that, there was no other way for money to change hands at the camel races. The religious prohibition on betting meant the races were a purer form of competition than western horseracing, with far less chance of them being rigged. And anyway the owners all wanted desperately to win.

It was impossible for me to draw conclusions from the racing

I saw that day. I kept a stopwatch on each race, but I had no yardstick to know whether the times being run were good, bad or indifferent. In fact, there wasn't much science at all around the races. They were a relatively uncomplicated affair with the Bedouin from different tribes simply competing to win, and having a wonderful get-together at the same time.

But in another way I took home—or rather, to the Hilton Hotel—a treasure-trove of information about what camels mean to this society and, importantly, to my paymasters. There were two societies here: the UAE for expat westerners and the UAE for the Emiratis. Someone had opened the door for me and allowed me to enter a rarely glimpsed world. And the UAE, it was clear, was run by camel men.

The relationship of Emiratis with the camel went deep. These animals were the glue that bonded the old and the new, and that needed to be preserved.

Five
Faster, stronger

As a regional town, Al Ain wasn't nearly on the same scale as expat hubs like Dubai and Abu Dhabi, where a newly arrived westerner would merge into the background with all the others. In the big centres of Dubai and Abu Dhabi the westerners lived in sealed-off compounds with each other for company; they might not ever actually work with an Emirati. When they shopped they could buy familiar brands from back home at big western-style supermarkets. They could get fast food from a KFC or dine at an upmarket restaurant, just like in London, Paris, New York or Sydney.

Consequently, it was possible for an expat to never actually meet and talk to the locals whose country they lived in. They were guest workers and it was largely an arm's length arrangement.

Not so in Al Ain. There were no grand shopping malls and giant supermarkets; life was on a more modest scale. The local shops were mostly small family concerns all in a row on the various street blocks of Al Ain, and that was where you bought your groceries, and your fruit and vegetables. Unusually, all the shops of a type were grouped together. There was the block for chemists, the block for tailors or for hardware or fabric shops and so on. Being a rural centre, you could get essentials for a farm, like hosepipes and drums of fertiliser. And when you went up the street you would be walking alongside the locals and sitting down to eat with them.

In Dubai and Abu Dhabi the expats would tool around in late model four-wheel drives or a new European saloon. In Al Ain you were more likely to see locals turning up in an old ute with three or four baby camels in the rear, alongside the Range Rovers and Landcruisers of the now well-off Bedouin.

Above all, Al Ain was a town for and by the people of the desert. It is one of the oldest continuously inhabited places in the world, stretching back perhaps four thousand years. The Bedouin, who had not so long ago roamed the sands and made small settlements here and there, were now clustered together near town in houses provided by the government. It was part and parcel of the UAE's transition away from the old desert culture and towards something more modern.

That gave Al Ain the feel of a frontier town, a place where you lived by the traditional rules of the desert rather than the more homogenised ways of a big, westernised city.

As an outpost town, Al Ain had been the launching pad for some of the great battles of Arab history, the place from which the ruling tribe had ridden off on their camels to repel tribal invaders from present-day Oman or Saudi Arabia. It was also a place that attracted its fair share of legendary characters, like the Eton-educated British adventurer Wilfred Thesiger, who crossed the vast expanse of the Empty Quarter by foot and camel with teams of young Bedouin Arabs in the 1940s and 1950s.

Only days after I arrived I came face to face with one of the huge figures from my university days in the corner of the Hilton bar: it was none other than my 'Zoo Vet' hero David Taylor, the man whose books I had devoured as a young student and who had inspired me to pursue a big life with the animals of the wild. This was one of those surreal moments in life; the last time I had seen David Taylor's face was on the cover of a book in my family home in Glenrowan, Victoria. I walked up and introduced myself.

David Taylor, too, had been drawn to Al Ain because of the animals. He recounted how he had been hired as head consultant to redevelop the Al Ain zoo. The ruling family had ambitions to make the local zoo the biggest and best in the Middle East and had sought out David to help make it a showcase for the region. I couldn't believe my luck.

No matter what I did, it seemed I couldn't escape wild things, and here they were on my doorstep. Al Ain's zoo held the regular range of African animals—gorillas, lions, giraffes and tigers. Improbably, given the extreme heat of the Arab Gulf, it also had a collection of penguins. But it was also home to a selection of desert animals you wouldn't necessarily find elsewhere, animals like the ibex and the oryx.

I have a rule of thumb that if you land in a country you've never been to, go to the zoo and you'll get a good idea of what's going on. Maybe it's a vet thing. Perhaps an accountant judges a country by how well it reconciles its ledgers, but I always believe you can judge a country by its zoos and the way it treats its animals. If you can't look after your animals, you can't look after your people.

It also tells you a lot about how a country is run. Singapore, for example, has a sensational zoo: well-kept and clean. Go to India and you'll see something entirely different. On one visit to Delhi's zoo I was standing outside the cobra cage, indulging my snake fascination. No-one else was around and one of the staff asked if I would like to see the giant cobra close-up, for a small fee. He brought me into the cage, got out a broom and began poking the sleeping snake. The next minute this mighty four-metre king cobra had reared up, head level with mine and hood in full flare. I said, 'I think I've seen enough.'

That episode told me you could make anything happen in India by passing on a bit of cash. In Havana's zoo, I have seen a local sitting inside the crocodile enclosure with a fishing rod in his hand. That was a sure sign of how tough it was to get by in Cuba.

So it boded well that David Taylor, the original great of the zoo vet world, was here. That chance encounter with my hero convinced me this was truly my destiny.

In fact, in out of the way Al Ain it seemed suddenly that all things were possible for a secret zoo vet like myself. When I walked through town and down to the markets I discovered a delicious surprise—or something quite alarming, depending on your perspective. Al Ain was home to a wildlife market, where you could acquire pretty much anything your heart desired: a cheetah, a baboon, snakes, lizards, a crocodile. Whatever took your fancy, it was there.

This was something you would never see in Australia; the law simply would not allow it. But the desert Arabs have a rich history of trading, bringing in all manner of goods from Africa and the rest of the Middle East, so animals were just part of that. I was still living at the hotel so couldn't take anything back from the markets with me. But I made a mental note of what was on offer for later, when the time came to turn our house under construction into a real Tinson home.

■ ■ ■

It didn't take long for word to spread amongst the local Bedouin that the western experts had arrived. Things might have been different if we'd been brought in, say, as engineers to build an airstrip. Jobs like that required knowhow that didn't exist in the UAE. The locals readily appreciated that there were things foreign experts knew that they didn't.

But camels were something else altogether. Our business was very much their business and it was hard for us to simply go about our work unnoticed. And the locals had every reason to be sceptical, even resentful. The Bedouin had developed an intuitive knowledge of their camels, which can only come from thousands of years of living together with the animals.

It was all very well to be parachuted in as the world's leading camel vet, as Heath had sold me, but what did I really know? I had up my sleeve this thing called 'western knowhow', but I was already aware that it was painfully inadequate. Sure, I had castrated Paddy McHugh's camels and been in charge of an endurance race, but they were outback Australian camels that had evolved in the wild to become big hulking things that could carry massive loads. The Arabian racing camels were a very different beast, only half the size of their Australian cousins and much more slender, like a greyhound.

The racing camels I'd seen were no wider than an average person at the shoulders. They had a tiny waist, and with this narrow waist they had very fine legs, more like the great Ethiopian runners. To get it in perspective, an adult female camel in the Middle East might weigh in at four hundred kilograms. By comparison, a decent-sized Australian camel is six to seven hundred kilograms while a racehorse is up to 550 kilograms.

The difference is that in Australia there had been no selective breeding, whereas the Bedouin Arabs have been breeding for speed and endurance, because they wanted to ride in battle or make a fast escape. In traditional times they needed to get across the desert quickly, so they were always looking for faster, stronger camels. It's been selective breeding all the way to produce a very fine-boned mix of speed and endurance.

I'd researched what I could on the health and ailments of camels but had found very few articles. One reason was that camels are so resilient there's been nothing much to write about. And of course, the camel had never attracted the interest of western vets in the way horses and cattle do. In fact, very little was known about them, full stop.

I also found virtually nothing in the literature to guide us on how certain drugs affected camels. We could extrapolate from other species, but that's highly fraught: an anti-inflammatory that gives good results with a horse can be very toxic in camels, as it turns out. In fact, when it comes to drug treatment, the camel is nearly always different. What happens in a horse or cow didn't necessarily apply. So it's no understatement to say that I was feeling my way in the dark when it came to the racing camels.

Mr Zuhair arranged for Hamza to take all us Australian vets—Doug, Geoff and me—to visit one of the Crown Prince's camel camps in the desert, a few kilometres outside town. In all there were fifteen camps spread around various places, as well as four breeding farms and over three thousand camels that we would have to get to know and work with.

The camp we were visiting held a herd of around a hundred camels kept in various enclosures that had been fenced off in a flat area of the desert. There were twenty or so camel handlers tending to the herd, filling feed boxes and water troughs, leading groups of camels from enclosure to enclosure. The men were from poorer countries, such as Pakistan, India, Bangladesh and Sudan. The youngest was probably about nineteen and the oldest maybe forty-five to fifty. The Pakistani men in particular would have grown up with camels and all the handlers lived here full-time, in quarters at the camp. They were here because it was a life that was better than what they could get in their own countries, which in a way applied to all of us.

We made for a small building near the camp entrance where we met the head trainer, a solid, no-nonsense Emirati man called Saeed bin Krause. Saeed was an Arab version of

Paddy McHugh: he lived and breathed the animals and had in him the spirit of the wild. But Saeed also drew on centuries of knowledge, because the Bedouin culture had developed around the resilience of the camel. It was literally man's best friend, if not saviour.

Saeed had been atop a camel from the age of two. He was reared with camels. As we wandered through the herd it seemed he had a sixth sense, which meant he knew how an animal was feeling that day, if it had energy or if there was an ailment which meant it wasn't quite itself.

He was typical of the Bedouin we would deal with, who had learned the ways of the camel from birth. These were men who had the ability to identify a camel from the imprint of a hoof in the sand and tell from that how many hours had passed since it had crossed the desert.

This first meeting was an eye-opener for all of us. Saeed had never met a western vet before. He would have been curious to know if we had something special to offer. At the same time I was wondering if we had anything to offer at all.

On this patch of dirt and with these beasts, Saeed was king. Even though we were here with the authority of the Crown Prince, for us to do our job effectively we needed the support and goodwill of trainers like Saeed and, indeed, the camel handlers themselves. And, as in thoroughbred horseracing, it was absolutely vital to get the relationship right between vet and trainer. There just had to be mutual respect.

However, the local Bedouin trainers didn't necessarily trust us. They weren't hostile to us, but they were resistant. There were camel doctors here who relied on a tradition that stretched back hundreds, if not thousands, of years. We were outsiders and brought with us new methods that were seriously at odds with those customs. It didn't matter to them that through us they would have access to some of our advanced medicines. They employed natural treatments that had been passed down through the ages and been validated by experience.

Prior to our arrival, the camels were treated with Bedouin cures. One of these, for example, involved putting a burn on an injury, by using a red hot poker, as a way of 'toughening' the leg, not unlike the practice of pin firing, which was used to treat racehorses in the west before it was stopped in the early 1980s because it was considered cruel. They were also using herbal medicines such as the desert purgative harem bush.

The Bedouin trainers were suspicious of even the most basic surgery. A simple procedure, like lancing an abscess, was regarded with great suspicion and required much discussion prior to permission being given to proceed. As far as the Bedouin were concerned, if it couldn't be given orally, it was suss.

There was also a real fear of reprisals should something go wrong. The animals were worth hundreds of thousands of dollars and were being trained for members of the ruling families. How to explain if a new drug or a medical procedure went wrong and destroyed the camel?

Language was another fundamental problem. The Bedouin trainers barely understood a word of English. And of course, we couldn't speak any Arabic, let alone the dialect of the desert. At one stage we tried to make light of the language barrier by having an English-speaking local translate some Australian colloquialisms—like 'don't come the raw prawn' or 'hit the frog and toad'—but the literal translations didn't quite hit the mark and the whole attempt fell flat. Yet it was essential that we should communicate our ideas on treatments as well as our plans for research. It was also vital that we learn from the trainers and benefit from their knowledge of camels in general.

All in all, it was pretty clear that this wasn't a matter of waltzing in with our medicine and taking over.

We raised this problem with Mr Zuhair. He heard what we and Saeed both had to say and, weighing up the arguments, decided that we needed to gain the confidence of the local Bedouin. They had to be convinced that our scientific approach worked. The solution was that before letting us loose on the Bedouin camels, we would have the chance to try out our techniques on twelve camels of our own.

At the same time we vets would have a go at being trainers for the rest of the camels and have the freedom to introduce new methods, as long as they didn't involve medicine. It wasn't part of the original brief, but this would give us time to get a feel for how the local camel experts worked. Simultaneously, we and our 'advanced' techniques were on trial with our own dozen.

It was a smart decision.

■ ■ ■

We were conscious that we were on probation and needed to make a mark. But while we felt the pressure to make quick progress, we were limited in the kind of scientific work we could do. At the moment we had nothing: no staff, no clinic. Just sand and the Hilton Hotel.

To get over the immediate language problem, Mr Zuhair assigned a full-time interpreter to us, a young man from Sudan called Bengawi. He had trained as an accountant, so he had to get up to speed with the language of the technical ideas we needed to impart.

We learned that the complex, when it was built, would be known as the Scientific Centre for Racing Camels. If our science was going to help make the Crown Prince's camels faster, then we would need the equipment and the backup to make that happen. We had firm plans as to what we wanted to do. Right from the early days it was important that we be able to monitor the health of our animals very closely. We needed to be able to give our trainers same-day blood reports and understand how certain markers in the blood matched up with performance. It was also critical to accurately diagnose disease in an animal, so as to provide the correct treatment.

Our first aim was to analyse blood samples from all our racing camels and create the basic physiological data that was absent in the region. This would require labs with specialised equipment and personnel.

During the course of the Great Australian Camel Race, I had to know the physical capabilities of every animal, for their sake as much as the humans. I was constantly monitoring the impact of exercise on the blood and the heart, so now we fed this existing data into our early physiological exercise work with the camels.

A key means for us to measure this would be using a treadmill, common for training horses but never before used for camels. This would mean assembling a team of professionals from overseas, including world experts in horse exercise physiology and human exercise physiology, and drawing on research about marathon runners, amongst other things. The aim was to design and build specialised treadmills for the project, robust enough to carry a four-hundred-kilogram beast. The treadmills would be fitted with oxygen masks for the camels, which would allow us to measure oxygen uptake under stress.

All this would take time. Until then, we knew we would be tested on the little things.

Apart from Heath, none of us had family here, which in some ways helped our cause. Being by ourselves we had little to do other than work, eat, sleep, and then do it all again, out there with the camels from four in the morning to get the heavy work done before the heat of the day.

Not knowing a whole lot about Arabian camels, we applied principles that we knew worked with training racehorses. One of the most critical first steps was something very basic: going out onto the track with a stopwatch to measure the time it took for a camel to complete the six to eight kilometres of a normal race. Timings had never mattered to the local trainers.

Winning the race was enough, and it didn't really matter if it took fifteen or eighteen minutes, so long as you won.

But we were looking at it from another perspective: we wanted the camel to run faster. Pretty soon the Bedouin trainers started saying these stopwatches weren't too bad after all and they began using them.

We also had a suspicion that the camels weren't doing much running between events. It was common for the trainers to get the camel handlers to take the camels out for a five- or ten-kilometre walk. One day we discreetly followed behind this 'training' in a car and discovered that the camels were being taken to the nearest big sand dune, whereupon the workers would tie up the camels and have a snooze.

So we visited the industrial area that housed the Crown Prince's workshop and garage, a set-up where we were able to get petrol between the hours of 6am and 1pm. There we made the acquaintance of a man called Yafour, an older Emirati who was able to conjure anything out of a bit of metal. We asked him to weld together a makeshift T-bar sulky, which we could put behind a car. Now we could have heaps of camels tied up behind the thing and drag them around for training.

We tried everything. The cattle prodder was introduced as a way to quickly get the camels into line for training; the idea of a small electric spark coming out of the end of a stick seemed to capture everyone's imagination. This led to an amusing incident with a sheikh who was keen to have one of these for himself. We presented him with a prodder from Australia and showed him how it worked by tapping the top of a table with it. *Zzzzt.* Out came an electric charge. But this didn't seem to satisfy the sheikh. He summoned an underling and told him to put out his hand. *Zzzzt.* The poor guy just about hit the roof. It seems the sheikh wanted to test out the limits before exposing his camel to anything awful.

Some ideas were weird and wonderful. With Heath's background as a horse man we decided we should have a go at transporting camels standing up. So we asked Yafour to fix us up with a truck with a hydraulic lifter on the back where the camels could walk onto the platform and be raised up. Unfortunately that one didn't take off because camels prefer to sit down. Indeed, they are designed to sit down, unlike horses, which are designed to stand up and have ligaments that lock their legs into that position. That's why camels have those wonderful external pads on their knees and their chests, so they can sit in the desert sands for days without getting bedsores. The pads also help protect them from the heat.

So some things worked and others didn't, but slowly we were revolutionising camel training. Most importantly, we got the attention of the locals and they were starting to see that we could get results.

We had a bit of fun with it, too. We named all our camels after famous Australians. There was Marjorie (Jackson), Betty (Cuthbert) and Shirley (Strickland). All the Bedouin came to know a pure white Sudanese camel we called Greg Norman, after the Great White Shark, who many of the locals had heard of. Greg and another camel we named Debbie (Flintoff-King) were always amongst the winners. And come race day we Australians always had a good old laugh to ourselves to hear the race caller bellow out 'Greg Norman' or 'Dame Edna' amongst the Arabic.

All the while, Mr Zuhair took a special interest in how things were going; with us living at the hotel, it was hard to avoid him. He would take up his position in the café like clockwork at 6pm every day and was a fund of helpful advice.

We were clearly under the spotlight. From time to time we would be visited by higher-ups in the local hierarchy, who had been sent to report back to the Crown Prince.

Heath Harris had a line that summed up life here perfectly: the UAE is like a giant film set, he would say, and you are only as good as your last movie. It captured the truth that, along with the good pay and conditions, there was a demand to produce the goods.

■ ■ ■

Being hired as the camel vet didn't mean that was all you would do. Part of the test in the early days was also to see how well we could build our relationships. We had to be flexible, prepared to do anything and everything when asked. And that's how I ended up crossing paths again with the mountain lion that had made such an impression at the welcome lunch.

It turned out that the prominent local who strolled in that day, with that elegant but deadly creature on a leash, was not its owner. He had borrowed it for the occasion from an Australian mate of ours called Kent who was working for the US defence company Raytheon, makers of the Patriot missile.

The mountain lion was a gift to Kent's family from the Crown Prince's half-brother. It's very hard to say no when a member of the ruling family offers you a gift, even something as unruly as a mountain lion. And having accepted it, it is equally hard to offload it. So what do you do?

Kent's solution was to keep him in the backyard, attached to a runner chain. That way it could at least have a bit of space, however limited, to stretch out its legs.

This gave rise to a terrible practical joke that I once played on our driver. Hamza had driven Doug and me up to Kent's house in Abu Dhabi for lunch one day and, in his customary way, said he would wait in the car until we were ready to return to Al Ain. I told him to come inside and join us to eat but he declined, pointing to a 'Beware of the dog' sign on the front of the house. I reassured Hamza, saying, 'Look, there are no dogs, okay? Come on in.'

Doug and I walked ahead. Meanwhile, Hamza locked the car and followed us along the pathway down the side of the house. Suddenly he looked across and saw this killer sprinting at him at sixty kilometres an hour. It hit the chain and stopped about a metre away from him. He stood there, completely frozen. 'Well,

Hamza,' I said, 'that's not a dog. That's a mountain lion.' I'm not sure that Hamza saw the funny side of it.

As it grew older, that sleek little mountain lion started getting a bit more rambunctious, until one day he bit off the tip of Kent's right earlobe. That wasn't great for Kent, but at least he now had a good enough reason to have a word with the sheikh and let him know the puma had become a bit of a handful. Kent proposed that the cat be sent to the zoo at Al Ain and the sheikh agreed.

And that's where I got involved, receiving a call asking if I would please do the honours. I jumped in my car with Doug and headed up to Kent's place, throwing in a blowpipe and a dart gun in case this manoeuvre called for my old sedating skills from the lion park days.

The mountain lion was still only ten months old and, having spent much of its life around humans, it was still just possible to handle him like you would an excited dog. I got Kent and a couple of others to hold and play with him while I quietly drew a couple of ccs of sedative drug into a syringe. I managed to slip a fine needle in without him noticing and fifteen minutes later he was out cold.

Doug and I took one end each and put him into the back of the Landcruiser, ready for the trip back from Abu Dhabi. Job well done—or so we thought. An hour or so later as we made it to the outskirts of Al Ain and were stopped at traffic lights the people in the car next to us started waving and pointing madly to the back of our car. We turned around to see the mountain lion now awake and attempting to scramble over the rear divider into the back seat.

Thankfully, though, he was still groggy. We figured we had just enough time to get to the Al Ain zoo, about ten minutes away across town, and dump the lion. But by the time we got there, it had gone 8pm and no-one would let us in.

Now we didn't know what to do. Here we were, feeling a bit ridiculous, with a dozy mountain lion on our hands, becoming more alert by the minute, and nowhere to take it. The only place to go was 'home' to the Hilton. We presented ourselves at reception and, using my best straight face, I asked if there might be an extra room available, for the mountain lion. The bloke at the desk just looked at us. We knew it was probably not out of the ordinary for someone to walk into the hotel with a cheetah or something similar, but maybe taking a room was a step too far.

We were still in negotiations when a call came through from the zoo. They must have heard we were working for the sheikh, so someone opened the zoo and we were able to get over quick smart and drop that mountain lion off before it was fully alert.

That's the problem with animals from the wild. They are, in the end, wild.

■ ■ ■

Our small group of Australians held regular brainstorming sessions where we looked at every possible angle to improve the performance of the Crown Prince's camels. We drew up a page with arrows going everywhere, and in the middle of it was Sheikh Khalifa.

Our ultimate benchmark was Dubai and, in particular, Sheikh Mohammed bin Rashid Al Maktoum, the son of the then Ruler of Dubai. At that point, Sheikh Mohammed was probably both the leading horse owner and the leading camel owner in the world. His facilities were absolutely world class and he had attracted the best Arab trainers.

We were left in no doubt about how intense the rivalry was between the two city-emirates of Dubai and Abu Dhabi. Though a mere 120 kilometres or so distant from each other, the two had only recently been joined together under one flag.

Three decades before, when I was a little kid running around the yard at St Ives, Abu Dhabi and Dubai had been at war over territory, a formal compromise only coming in the late 1970s. In the desert timeframe, this was like yesterday.

There was no getting around some very basic arithmetic. It came down to this: Sheikh Mohammed of Dubai had ten thousand camels—and the Crown Prince of Abu Dhabi had three thousand. Just working the straight percentages, if you assume that two per cent of all your camels are going to be champions, Sheikh Mohammed was always going to be ahead of us.

For all the marvellous new training techniques we'd introduced, we were still fiddling at the edges. We were on the lookout for the one big idea.

It was Heath Harris who, in typical fashion, came up with a belter. Heath is one of those people who left school at fourteen but has more ideas than anybody I've ever met. There might have been a few weird ones but, out of ten, maybe three would be rippers.

'Why don't we just try embryo transfer?' Heath ventured. The rest of us highly trained vets were dumbfounded: this was something that had never been done before.

Embryo transfer is a tricky business. You have to be able to superovulate an animal so it produces a large number of eggs. We vets knew that this had not proven possible with horses. At the very best a mare might produce three or four eggs when stimulated, but this was not enough for a reproductive program. And we had assumed the same would apply to camels. To which Heath said, 'Well, too bad—I've already told the Crown Prince that we can. So we're going to do it.' Nothing like making scientific history on the run.

There was an ironclad logic to what Heath was saying. We needed a bigger herd and the way to do that was to breed *faster* from the existing herd. Yes, you could go out and simply buy more camels. But the beauty of embryo transfer is that you can breed from the gene pool of your best camels.

It was also a way to increase the number of babies a good female might produce in its lifetime. With a gestation period of thirteen to fourteen months, the camel is incredibly slow reproductively. As well, a female racing camel might only have six years or so of reproductive life, given that it is customarily raced up to the age of ten or twelve years. The female is superior to the male when it comes to racing. It's not just that they are faster: the males tend to be more temperamental and harder to deal with. Hence the females have longer racing lives. We did the numbers and figured out that if embryo transfer worked, we could produce the equivalent of twenty years of breeding in just one year. It was clear that this could hold the key to catching up with our rivals. We could breed selectively from our best animals and try to speed up the whole process of genetic selection. The race just might be won in the lab.

We couldn't experiment on the Abu Dhabi camels, some of which were worth a million dollars or more. The risk was too great that something could go wrong. The only way we could test Heath's theory was to experiment on camels that were available in large numbers and it wouldn't matter if things went wrong. This, naturally, pointed to the wild camels of Australia.

We had also heard on the grapevine that Dubai was considering the idea of collecting Australian camels for their own research purposes. We didn't believe that this would include embryo transfer because it was such a left-of-field idea but there were other reasons they might want to look closely at them. So the competition was on.

We put the case to Mr Zuhair and he agreed. Given the interest Dubai was now showing in Australian camels, our operation was to be conducted in secret. Only a handful of the most senior Emiratis would know the details of our moves to pioneer reproductive technology for camels.

One of those was Aylan bin Abdallah Al Muheiri, who had been a bodyguard of Sheikh Khalifa. Now head of the Crown

Prince's personal security and a trusted confidante, Aylan had good knowledge of camels.

We had been only been in Al Ain for eight months. Patti, Katya, Erica and little Natalia had been there for half that time and we were all shacked up in the Hilton while our family home was being completed The next thing I was on a plane heading for the desert of Western Australia, and then to my old stomping ground in western Queensland to catch wild camels. If this worked, it would be a world first and a major breakthrough in our quest to be the best.

It was hard to tear myself away from the family again, but I imagined it was only going to be for four or so weeks. Once again, that was not the way it turned out.

Six
The unexpected

Heath was a man for big ideas, but I was the vet with the expertise in camels. The responsibility was squarely on my shoulders. And Heath had raised an almighty expectation.

But I was determined to make this work so right at the start I brought on board an old university mate of mine, Dr Angus McKinnon, who had done pioneering embryo transfer work with cattle and horses. But would the same principle apply with camels? The plan was that we would conduct our experiment from go to whoa in Australia and, should it work, we would then replicate it in Al Ain.

I met up in with Angus in Perth and we flew first to Port Hedland on the north-western coast of Western Australia, and then another couple of hundred kilometres inland to Marble Bar.

First we needed to round up wild camels and we did it on an industrial scale: three hundred in all. To do this we required light planes to go camel spotting, and helicopters and groups of vehicles to herd them into fenced-off holding pens.

Embryo transfer is a delicate scientific procedure that needs to be done in laboratory conditions, using very advanced equipment. It involves injecting a female with hormonal drugs to stimulate the production of eggs then, using ultrasound, monitoring the effects to see how many egg-carrying follicles are produced and to determine the best time for mating.

Once the eggs are fertilised the embryos are flushed from the female, isolated and cleaned before being implanted in other females as surrogates. This means you need to have other female camels ready and primed to accept an embryo. In other words, they need to be hormonally synchronised using drugs, with their bodies tricked into thinking they are pregnant. Timing is everything if the implanted embryo is to turn into a pregnancy.

As far as breeding faster camels goes, using embryos from your best female racing camel with your best male is much more likely to result in the right genes. Then the lower quality females carry the embryos and give birth, which frees up your high-quality female to continue racing—and puts your lower quality females to good use giving birth to future champions.

That was the theory, anyway, but we were working with a hundred unknowns because of the limited knowledge of camel reproductive cycles. All we knew was that they were not like humans or cattle or horses, where the female releases an egg at regular times in a cycle.

Angus tried out different hormone regimes to discover what worked with the camel. We injected them with moderate doses and then overdoses to establish boundaries. We explored the reproductive anatomy of the camel to determine how we needed to adapt established embryo transfer techniques. The anatomy of a camel's cervix, for example, is different to the horse or the cow.

We discovered that the best way to collect semen was to anaesthetise the male and use electro-ejaculation to stimulate the production of sperm, because camels aren't necessarily co-operative when it comes to mating.

Within a month we knew we were onto something major. The fertility drugs had produced thirty to forty eggs per camel which were ready to be fertilised. It was a huge number and something we could never have expected; a cow might produce fifteen to twenty eggs and a horse only three or four at the very best. The results were beyond our wildest hopes, and we were the first in the world to do it. I reported back to Heath and I could hear the relief in his voice from ten thousand kilometres away.

This was our Eureka moment. We knew right then that we were in business.

■　■　■

Unfortunately, though, this standout success is not what I remember most about this trip to Australia.

Two weeks into our embryo work at Marble Bar I took a call late at night from Heath, on the line from Al Ain. I knew instantly that something was very wrong.

There was no easy way to break the news. 'Alex,' Heath said, 'Natalia has been found dead.' Our baby had stopped breathing and no-one knew exactly why.

Natalia was just nine months old.

I couldn't quite comprehend what Heath was telling me. For a moment I thought he might be having a lend of me. I was numb with disbelief. How was this possible, again? When I had left her in Al Ain a fortnight before there was nothing wrong with her. For all I knew she was a million dollars.

Heath told me that Natalia was sleeping in her cot when Patti went out to do some shopping. About half an hour later our housemaid had discovered her, apparently lifeless, and had raced into the office next door to get Heath. But nothing could be done. She died on the way to hospital.

Having left the family behind in Australia and then leaving them for a second time, I had spent only a few months with her. Now she was dead. The idea that we could have lost our second baby was so outside the bounds of reality that I just didn't get it. I was numb.

We packed up the lab and I travelled back down to Perth with Angus to make arrangements for Natalia's funeral. Forty-eight hours later Patti and the girls arrived at Perth airport with a tiny coffin bearing our baby. Heath and his wife, Chrissie, came along from Al Ain with them. We were still none the wiser about what exactly had happened; it ended up being called sudden infant death syndrome. Like Anya three years before, it was another unexplained event. I just wanted more information.

Natalia's funeral passed in a blur. It felt unreal to be sitting with Patti and the girls, looking on at this tiny coffin and knowing our baby girl was inside. There was nothing quite like seeing that tiny coffin coming down the aisle, let alone for the second time. It started. Then it was over. I felt disconnected from everything unfolding around me, as though I wasn't even there and this was happening to someone else. I was immune from any feeling, so much so that I didn't even cry. What kind of father doesn't cry at his own baby's funeral? I still have a lot of trouble with the fact that I didn't shed even one tear. That is something that has stayed with me all these years later.

■　■　■

Everything about Natalia's funeral was surreal. None of us had any attachment to Perth: no family, no past, no memories. We held the funeral there for no other reason than it was the closest city to where I was working. Where was home, anyway?

Not Tweed Heads anymore. And certainly not Sydney or Melbourne, which I had left years ago. If home is the place where you are most comfortable then home was wherever the camels were.

As a family we couldn't be apart right now, so Patti and I decided all four of us would stick together. I had unfinished business with the embryo transfer project, and to be honest there was no better place to be than on Corunna Downs Station, near Marble Bar: out in the middle of the desert with the camels and nobody else, maybe we could try to get our heads around what had happened.

We really isolated ourselves for the first two or so weeks. I didn't want people milling around with their sympathy, as well meaning as it was. We were with close friends like Angus as well as some Emiratis who had flown out for the project. I found it better to keep working with the camels than to stop, think and maybe fall to pieces. So, yes, I distracted myself from the whole thing.

I have grown to like deserts because they are so completely isolated and isolating. You can get yourself into a place that allows you to feel insignificant in this huge expanse. Wherever you look, there is nothing and nobody.

There is also something comforting about being in a desert with camels. Humans aren't meant to be in the desert but, as long as you have a camel, you are safe. So being with camels in these incredible expanses gives a real sense of belonging, especially in the Australian desert, with only deafening silence and the vast emptiness of the Milky Way above you. At no point can you feel less significant.

What are the odds of losing not just one but two babies? And for this to happen not in war or famine but in the safety of home, sleeping in their cot? The odds seemed greater than the number of stars in the sky, twinkling down at you in the dead, black silence of a desert night. I occasionally allowed the reality of what had happened to creep in. We had lost

Anya, done the camel race across Australia when I survived for weeks on end buzzing on adrenalin and three hours' sleep a night. We had another baby, moved to the Middle East. Then we lost Natalia. For three years we'd spun from one life-changing event to another.

Bit by bit, Patti and I were gathering ourselves together to do what we had done with Anya: to put a brave face on it all and carry on. Soon enough, if a stranger were to look at either of us, they would never have guessed what we'd been through.

I often look back at Lindy Chamberlain and the death of her baby, Azaria, in the desert. People were so quick to judge her because she looked 'hard'. In other words, she wasn't a weeping, emotional mess. But I think Patti and I were a bit like that to the outside world. I could understand Lindy Chamberlain's 'cold' reaction, which meant she was attacked for apparently being an unfeeling bitch. Why should she be criticised? Does anyone really know how they would react until it happened to them? Thankfully, very few people will ever know what it is like to lose a baby, but that doesn't stop them making judgements. We're all meant to die before our children.

As part of coming to terms with our tragedy, we carried Natalia's ashes with us to Patti's parents' farm at Healesville, outside Melbourne. It was a place that held a special significance for us. There, on the top of a hill, was a beautiful, peaceful spot that we knew only too well. Patti's father's ashes already lay there under a large, spreading tree. It was also where we had spread Anya's ashes. Now Natalia would join her. Many years later I returned to fix a brass plaque to the tree, with a poem in memory of our babies.

Our family emerged, collectively, from our shell shock and continued on back into the world. We travelled up to the Top End to make a base at Buckingham Downs Station near Boulia, the Queensland town that had been the scene of our worst times in the Great Australian Camel Race.

My old mate Paddy McHugh was now on board and in charge of this second leg of our mission. It was time to go camel chasing again. We needed a herd of camels to take back to Al Ain for the second phase of our embryo transfer research: using Australian camels to test out our techniques in Al Ain. We hired a number of helicopters to fly out from Mount Isa to find camels at Buckingham Downs, a spread of more than 300,000 hectares. The station was home to hundreds of wild camels and I knew from the Great Australian Camel Race that this part of the country had produced the best racing stock.

It was an exhilarating, adrenalin-charged exercise with a team of micro-helicopters turning on a sixpence as they manoeuvred wild camels through the dust and the dirt. The rotor blades were kicking up massive clouds of red sand as the camels skittered and attempted to gallop off in different directions. Paddy was fearless, doing what he does best. At one stage he leapt from a helicopter to get on top of a beast that was proving tricky and then bulldogged it into a corral.

We managed, finally, to herd thirty-two braying, kicking camels into a holding pen, fortunately without mishap. Paddy's job now was to train them so they would be ready to be loaded on a plane in Darwin in a couple of months' time for the trip to Al Ain aboard the Crown Prince's private Airbus, which had been specially fitted out to transport camels.

I also tossed in a Staffordshire bull terrier, who I called Rolley, just to make me feel more at home in the UAE.

Seven
Harry the Camel

We left Paddy to it and arrived back in Al Ain as a gang of four again, in the full fifty-plus degree heat of August.

We did our best to be normal, first busying ourselves getting Katya and Erica ready for the start of the new school year. I got cracking on work at the camel centre, which was nearly complete with the labs and equipment we needed to start some serious blood work.

It was as though the move back helped to draw a line under our tragedy. It brought us closer together, but Patti and I didn't talk about it. We had gone from nearly losing Katya, to losing Anya and then losing Natalia. Maybe we should have gone to therapy, but we didn't. We elected not to look into the chasm of despair beneath us. I think subconsciously I had a morbid dread that I could completely unravel if I allowed myself to really think about it too deeply. A survival instinct kicked in because I might well have collapsed in a heap.

And again, as if to show that life goes on, we soon found out that Patti was pregnant again. This was wonderful news—at least, it should have been. But I was worried. We had been fed a line that there was a familial genetic strain for sudden infant death syndrome, or SIDS, apparently based on research by a specialist. It set me off collecting cases to try to make sense of what had happened.

The term SIDS is used to apply to the unexplained death of children less than twelve months old. Although there has now been a dramatic decline in its incidence, at the time this was happening to us it was the leading cause of death in Australia for babies up to one year of age. It normally happened when a baby was sleeping and most often between the hours of midnight to 9am. There were many theories about the contributing factors: from cigarette smoke, to sleeping in the same bed as the parents, to having been born premature. However, around this time researchers discovered that if a baby slept on their back it was the single biggest step you could take to avoid SIDS, and that discovery led to a huge drop in the number of cases.

But most alarming to me at the time of our turmoil were the statistics. In Japan there was a one in ten thousand chance of a baby dying from SIDS. In the United States it was one in two thousand. The way I looked at it, we had experienced two cases and a near miss with Katya. If you take the US statistics, the chances of that happening three times in one family was eight billion to one. On the Japanese statistics it was a quadrillion to one. And suddenly you go, 'Fuck! They're crazy numbers.' Really, you've got much more chance of winning lotto.

All the while, I was thinking, is this new baby going to be part of the pattern playing out here? Are we going to have more 'genetic' problems? What in hell is going on?

■ ■ ■

Word came that the President of the United Arab Emirates, Sheikh Zayed, had been asking questions about how those Australians were going with the embryo transfers. He had apparently taken time out during a state visit to Japan to ring our boss, Mr Zuhair.

This was one of those good news/bad news scenarios. On the one hand we were blown away that the leader of the country would have our breeding program top of mind—it showed us how everything kept coming back to camels. On the other hand, it reminded us of the pressure we were under to produce the goods.

We had been hired to work with the Crown Prince's camels, but of course what is good for the son is good for the father. And what is good for the father is good for the emirate of Abu Dhabi. And what is good for Abu Dhabi is good for the UAE. In fact, it's just good, full stop.

Thankfully, we were able to report to Mr Zuhair that the news from Australia was very promising. On top of the success with superovulating the females, Angus McKinnon's team had completed a large number of successful embryo transfers with the wild camels in Marble Bar. The good thing is you don't need to wait long to know if a camel is pregnant, nor do you need to do any ultrasounds as you would with a horse. After twelve to fourteen days, if the female is pregnant her tail rises reflexively when she is placed near a male. It's pretty obvious. The final phase was to see how many of those pregnancies would become live births. We were very confident that most of them would, but you never know until you know.

The next step would be to take the science we had developed in Australia and apply it in the UAE, experimenting first with the Australian camels we'd rounded up at Buckingham Downs and which were to be freighted over. We would further refine our reproductive techniques with them as a final check before being let loose to use our technology on the Crown Prince's precious herd.

During all this time we had not yet met our ultimate employer, the Crown Prince. We had met his brothers as well as other notables, who were clearly his eyes and ears on the project, but not the man himself.

Word would certainly have spread that even the small changes we had made to training had made a difference. Our experimental group of twelve camels had picked up some wins at minor races around the country, mainly because they were fitter than the others.

On one of those occasions Doug and I had been due to meet the Crown Prince's son, who had arranged a special trip to see the new breed of camels in action. Unfortunately we had stayed way too late at a party the night before that had been hosted by Mr Zuhair's son. We were due at the track by 5.30am, but we'd slept in and only arrived at around 7am, after the races had finished. This was a scary moment: if there is one thing you must never do it is keep a member of the royal family waiting. We rushed out to the track and were guided to where the Crown Prince's son was hosting a gathering of local notables, sitting around a fire and having coffee in the cool of the morning. There was lots of security and lots of guns.

We presented ourselves sheepishly, fully expecting a rebuke for this serious lapse in protocol. I had rehearsed a line that I hoped might warm the situation. Using my basic Arabic, I apologised both for being late and for the quality of my Arabic, explaining that I could only talk about camels and women. 'What else is there?' the Crown Prince's son shot back in English and broke out into a big laugh. Fortunately for us, our camels had performed out of their skins and won several of the races, so the Crown Prince's son was very happy indeed. The kinship of the camel, it seemed, trumped everything.

Now, most likely because of our achievements in Australia, we were suddenly to meet the Crown Prince himself, Sheikh Khalifa. Such invitations are not made lightly. All those in the chain that led from the Crown Prince down needed to be satisfied that we were worthy of the honour; their reputations ride on getting their judgements right. Powerful men like the Crown Prince rely on the judgement of their gatekeepers, and the gatekeepers rely on the continuing trust of the powerful, such as the Crown Prince.

The invitation to meet the Crown Prince was therefore hugely significant. The occasion was Eid, the celebration that follows the end of the month of Ramadan. Eid is a period of rejoicing and eating after a month of dawn-to-dusk fasting, when you deny yourself earthly pleasures to be closer to God. The occasion of Eid is a special time in Islamic life when families gather together, something akin to Christmas and New Year for Christians.

The event was to be held at the royal family's palace, which occupied an entire block in the centre of Al Ain. The palace was surrounded by high walls, guarding the privacy of the ruling family. Even taking a photograph of the walls—let alone the palace inside—was strictly forbidden. The invitation was extended to all the Australians at the camel research centre—Heath, Doug, Geoff and me. I scrambled to get hold of a suit and tie.

On arrival we were ushered directly into an anteroom at the front of the palace reception area, but on the way through we got a quick glimpse of the inside of the meeting hall. It was huge, with high ceilings, gold chandeliers and a Persian rug running the length of the room. In the distance, at the very end, were ceremonial gold-braided chairs, and above them hung a massive photo of Sheikh Zayed, the President of the United Arab Emirates and father of Sheikh Khalifa, the Crown Prince. It was opulence on a scale none of us had seen before and we let out a collective, 'Holy shit.'

We were given the brief instruction that, when called, we should walk all the way to the end and greet the Crown Prince. But that was all. In the meantime we would wait in this room.

We waited. And we waited. It was a long, long time, maybe an hour and a half. Looking through the doorway of our room we were able to catch a glimpse of dignitaries as they arrived to have their cars parked. One by one a who's who of the UAE's most powerful men stepped past us. Some I recognised from television as government ministers. Many were wearing fine silk robes in black or gold over the top of the standard white cotton robes of the Gulf, a sign of their status. We were in no doubt that here was the very centre of power in the United Arab Emirates: the intricate web of family and old friendships, forged through tribal bonds and ancient battles. Now these business leaders, other sheikhs and VIPs from Al Ain made up the ruling elite of the nation.

Protocol dictated that each enter the room and walk the length of the vast Persian rug to greet His Highness. As each one arrived, all others in the room would stand. And, having met the Crown Prince, each would then take their place on one of the two hundred chairs lined up along each side of the room, after shaking the hand of every person who had already arrived. It was highly formal and ritualised, but at the same time there was the easy familiarity of people who had grown up with each other.

More and more people arrived. Then finally it was our turn to enter.

We got up, walked around the corner and, with our first step onto the Persian rug, four hundred Emiratis in ceremonial dress rose as one from their chairs. There, at the very end of the room, beneath the huge portrait of his father and flanked by giant UAE flags, sat Sheikh Khalifa. The walk was perhaps fifty metres, but it felt more like five hundred. The whole room remained standing as we made our way, three western suits in a sea of robes, until we finally stood face to face with our boss, the Crown Prince. We were briefly introduced, the Crown Prince nodding and taking us in. Then it was over and we returned the length of the room, this time shaking everyone's hand along the way.

We were the last of the guests to be presented, and as soon as that was over we were led into another room, where we sat on the floor for the feast. Today, seated in a small group with our camel bosses Mr Zuhair and Aylan Al Muheiri, we were being given the ultimate honour as we were joined by Sheikh Khalifa, with our interpreter, Bengawi, placed between us and His Highness. He asked how we were enjoying living in Al Ain and how our families were adjusting, but most of all he was keen to hear how the embryo transfer program was progressing.

We had made it to the inner sanctum of Arabia.

■ ■ ■

Baby Madeline came into the world twelve months after we had lost Natalia. What should have been a wonderful event was tempered by a corrosive anxiety: what if it happened again?

After what we had been through, of course, Madeline became probably the most spoilt, fussed-over child in existence. We took no chances. There were not one but two baby monitors on her continuously, so we could be sure that she was still breathing. Even with that we carried out constant checks. We slept with one eye open, never feeling completely sure if Madeline would survive the night or not.

Fortunately for me I am a very positive person; that's probably what has got me through everything, really. Without that, I think things could have been very different. I see what has happened to other people under similar circumstances and think, Jesus, how come I didn't spin off the edge? Looking back, it's amazing I didn't unravel. I just kept saying: 'I'm fine, I'm fine, I'm fine.'

I think of myself as a strong person. I'm not given to making excuses for my failures or when things go wrong. I look at my dad's life and all the horror he saw, yet he never went on about it and managed to live a normal life when he came to

Australia. Dad was from a generation that didn't complain, and he was also very British in that stiff-upper-lip way. Sure, he loved us, but he would never say so. That was my model of what a dad was and did.

And when you look at the kind of vet I became, there was nothing sentimental about it. I loved the wild animals most, the ones that have the sharpest survival instincts. I think I was always in love with the qualities of resilience, strength, self-sufficiency and a will to survive. Having always resisted the touchy-feely approach to things, later in life I've looked more closely at grief and advice on how to handle it. It turns out my reactions were a textbook case on what not to do. Here's a brief list of some of the things you can do wrong in situations like ours:

- avoid emotions
- be overactive leading to exhaustion
- use alcohol or other drugs
- make unrealistic promises to the deceased
- have unresolved grief from a previous loss
- resent those who try to help.

I could say 'yes' to just about every one of those, except for the alcohol and drugs.

I also wonder if living in the UAE was part of my therapy. It is so diverse, so changing, so challenging and stimulating. When you've got all of that going on, you haven't got time to sit in the corner and say, 'Woe is me.' Maybe if I had been back in Australia and just doing the same old stuff, I might have felt the emptiness more and life might have been very different. It's hard to know.

In a way, I guess I did undertake some therapy. Without making a conscious decision, I started playing around with drawing. I found it therapeutic to spend time immersed in my own thoughts, pencil and paper in hand. Eventually, out of the lines and curves I was drawing emerged a character. It was a camel who I called Harry—Harry the Lazy Camel, named in honour of my father, Harry Tinson. I turned the Harry drawing into a T-shirt design and then started doing illustrations and words for a children's book, with Harry the Lazy Camel as the central character.

My illustrations were sparse, like the desert itself. Harry's shape mimicked the soft, wind-sculpted curves of the sand dunes. He was an elegant creature and carried himself with a certain nonchalance. Harry liked the simple things in life, like curling up in the warm sun and sleeping. He entertained thoughts of being something else, like a racing camel or a wild Australian camel or some entirely different creature from wild Arabia, like a falcon or an oryx. But in the end he was just happy being himself.

I dedicated my first book to Madeline and certainly at the time believed I was doing this for our new baby. But in hindsight I think I was really retreating into a private world that allowed me to escape the trauma of loss.

For my second book I developed half a dozen new animal friends for Harry, including Carl the Racing Camel, Basil the Bactrian (two-humped) Camel and Felicity the Flamingo. The story went that Harry was unhappy because he didn't know the date of his birthday, so he went looking for answers from his friends. They didn't know either, but one day they decided to hold a surprise birthday party for him. Harry, of course, was asleep, so his friends placed a party hat on his head, a cake with candles next to his nose and presents all around him. He woke to find all his friends waiting for him. It was the best day in Harry's life.

This book was dedicated to Anya and Natalia. I penned an inscription: 'For Anya and Natalia, who never knew a birthday.'

Harry the Camel took the place of going to therapy, which I probably should have done. Indeed, Harry was to become an obsession.

Eight
Home, sweet home

Everything had moved incredibly fast, not just for me but my whole family. It was like riding the big dipper: one moment I was up on a professional high, the next I was dropping down into the emotional depths. I was the luckiest person in the world and at the same time the unluckiest.

In my work there were exhilarating breakthroughs along with heady, adrenalin-charged moments of walking through doors into a new culture. It was so alien, and sometimes scary. All was new; 'normal' barely existed.

But as a family, we needed anchors. And, being a Tinson family, that meant turning our desert house into a Tinson home.

Rolley, the Staffordshire bull terrier, was just the start. Staffies aren't everyone's cup of tea, but for us they were a family favourite. Patti had grown up with bulldogs, which have a similar temperament. Staffies are strong, determined little dogs, all muscle and grunt. Yes, they are part of the pit bull terrier breed and they can be pugnacious. But they are only dangerous if you don't treat them well. Otherwise they are intelligent, incredibly loyal dogs.

After Rolley we introduced a cute little Siamese kitten who we christened Baldrick. He and Rolley used to play together and generally hang out. Invariably, when we came home, they'd be curled up together on the front doorstep.

Our house adjoined the camel centre office complex and its holding pens, so we also had 150 or so camels in our backyard at any one time. Before long we introduced two magnificent purebred Arabian stallions into the mix, courtesy of a British friend of ours who was working for the royal stables. Mr Zuhair came to the party and organised for a couple of stables to be built next to the camels. The horses needed a lot of work, which was great because it meant the girls had to be disciplined with the brushing, feeding and exercise. This was important. Like most expat families in the Gulf, we had live-in home help, so there was a real risk that our kids would grow up with everything being done for them. Katya and Erica worked with the horses to turn them into showjumpers—not what they are bred for, but the girls stuck at it nevertheless.

Between the dog, the cat, the camels and the horses, we had the makings of the sort of home the girls had been used to in Australia. All we needed now were the wild things.

Living on the edge of the desert meant that the wildlife of the sands would often come to us. One surprise we found at the rear of our small garden was Arab desert hedgehogs, the smallest of the hedgehog family. Rolley was particularly attracted to these little beasts, but they had a great protective mechanism—they would immediately wrap themselves into a spikey little ball and become impossible to catch. Though of course that didn't stop Rolley from trying again and again.

We would also find the odd gerbil, a tiny little thing also known as the desert rat, hopping into our patch. This too provided something for Rolley and Baldrick to get excited about.

But our most interesting house guest, hands down—and the only one that ever fazed the girls—was Boris the camel spider. The camel spider is a massive creature, around twenty to twenty-five centimetres across; you get an idea of the size if you spread your fingers out and then put your hands side by side. Not only does it have a large body, it is also quite hairy, which is why it is known as the sheep of the desert. It was one of the weirdest beasts I'd seen and I was completely fascinated by them.

Actually we had quite a few camel spiders, but Boris was the standout: the biggest, meanest camel spider you've ever seen. It wasn't poisonous, but it was terrifying nonetheless. In the early days, before we knew much about the camel spider, driving out from our house we'd literally see Boris's shadow run across the driveway. That's how big and mean they are. Instead of two fangs they have four, which makes their bite more like a car crusher.

When I first found Boris in the garden, I cornered him and put him into a two litre ice-cream container, then plonked him into a disused aquarium. We'd toss him snacks to devour; Boris would demolish a fifteen-centimetre scorpion in about three seconds. He ate mice. Boris even ate other camel spiders. Anything you threw in, Boris would crunch, munch and swallow. The locals couldn't understand why we would keep Boris and his ilk in our house. Bedouin lore has it that these spiders sneak up on camels, anaesthetise them and then eat pieces out of them. They were scared witless by them.

When you don't know the desert, it's almost impossible to imagine that it could contain any life at all. It is a very different environment to the forest I grew up with as my backyard, with its treasure-trove of snakes and reptiles. But the desert, too, holds hidden treasures, if you know where and how to look. There is an elegant simplicity about the desert: a vast tableau of endless golden sand set against a big, brilliant blue sky. It's easy to believe you are the only living thing there. But if you get out of your four-wheel drive and walk slowly, you'll find the tell-tale signs of life. I learned from my forays into the desert that it is in fact best to head off on a camel. With their slow, rhythmic movement you soon become at one with the pace of desert life and start to see more clearly the wildlife that inhabits it.

Look carefully and you will see how the sand tells its own story. Here a snake has slithered across the grains of sand, leaving a smooth, flat trail in its wake. Or there the small, choppy imprint of a lizard's clawed feet, which have skittered across the sands. It's about training your eye and heightening awareness for a different form of wildlife. By concentrating your gaze really hard, you might just spot the eyeballs of the saw-scaled viper, a snake that buries itself by pushing its body up and out against the sand. This creates a trough in which it can sink below the surface, like a submerging submarine. All that will be left are the eyes, which are set high on top of its head.

The wildlife of the desert has adapted to its environment in much the same way that snakes and lizards have adapted to the Australian bush. Rather than tones of grey and brown, the desert animals have beige, creamy colourings, which make them hard to spot against the sand. And of course a lot of them only come out at night to escape the heat of the day. Most of the time you'll simply miss a desert snake or a lizard; it will feel your presence and quickly wriggle away under the sand as you approach. Their territory is different and they have adapted to quickly drill down into little holes in the sand. Desert snakes and lizards are generally much smaller than their Australian cousins for the simple reason that there is not as much wildlife to feast on. And unlike Australia, you are unlikely to find a deadly snake in the desert.

The most unpleasant desert reptile I have come across is an evil-looking character called the dabb lizard. This is a stocky lizard, like a cross between a bearded dragon and a stump-tailed lizard. The dabb is a truly ugly little beast and it has a ferocious bite; if it latches onto something it just doesn't let go, so you have to be extremely careful with it. Despite my willingness as a boy to keep all manner of poisonous snakes in my home, when it came to the dabb I thought better of it. It is popular in the Arabian Gulf as a delicacy and Emirati boys enjoyed hunting the dabb, so much so that it threatened to become extinct.

One of my favourite reptiles was a remarkable little lizard called the blue agama, which puffs itself up and changes colour from red to an iridescent blue when it senses danger. This bright colouring is common for animals from Africa, which is indeed the usual home of the blue agama. They are sociable creatures and they like to hang out in groups, so we acquired enough of them to keep each other company.

Some of my favourite new pets were hand-me-downs. Now and then I would get a call from Mr Zuhair or other locals I knew, wondering if I might please find a pet snake or a lizard for the children of a sheikh. I would head up to a shop in Dubai and buy something harmless like a corn snake; they are good as kids' pets because they aren't huge, have a docile nature and hardly ever bite. They are also very easy to look after.

I also got the occasional request for something more on the wild side, like a boa constrictor. They are impressive snakes but the boa can have a painful bite, especially if it's a large one, though it is rarely dangerous to humans. The thing about the boa constrictor is that it will strike when it feels there is a threat, so invariably it wouldn't be long before I got another call to say the snake had bitten little so and so—please come and get rid of it.

I was more than happy to oblige as the unofficial snake procurer because, as a kid, having snakes had sparked my lifelong interest in animals of the wild. I think every kid should have that chance.

A friend of ours living nearby had acquired a macaw from the local market. I don't mind admitting I was jealous. They are beautiful birds and for a while I toyed with getting one for our home. They are real characters but they are also very difficult to handle, more like a monkey than a standard bird. They have a big beak and my mate's macaw put it to use by chewing the piano, the upholstery and the electrical wiring. Another reason not to take on a macaw is that they live a very long time, up to seventy or eighty years, so they will more than likely outlive you, which means you have to make provision for them in your will. Apart from all that, as a rule I am opposed to keeping birds in captivity because they suffer by being confined. Snakes and lizards, on the other hand, are not intelligent enough to know they are in a small space. Normally they will curl up in a corner and believe this is their world. And snakes, particularly, are easy to care for. They only need to eat every two weeks or so.

Bit by bit, snakes and lizards took their places inside our home. It was far too hot to keep them outdoors, so I placed them in various aquariums around the house. So it looked at last like Katya, Erica and Madeline would be growing up with their own private menagerie of exotic beasts. Erica even made her own contribution when, as a ten-year-old, she accompanied me out to a camel camp and went off poking around by herself. After a while she turned up with a sandfish lizard in her hands, looking for all the world like a seasoned reptile hunter.

We now had animals aplenty for the kids, and most days they were outside messing around with the horses and the camels. I decided that, as a finishing touch, I needed to have a sign made up for the entrance to our driveway to warn drivers to slow down, so I went back down to the Crown Prince's workshop to see Yafour with his bits of metal and welding machine. He had worked miracles knocking together the machinery we needed to train the camels, but now I had a simple request: I wanted a sign, please, in English and in Arabic.

I carried it home, drilled some holes on the gate at the entrance to the driveway and fixed it on tight. Yafour had done a beautiful job, using white lettering on a red-for-danger background: 'WARNING! Reduce speed. Children and camels around', it announced.

This, finally, was home, sweet home.

Nine
Dicing with danger

As an Australian vet in a town of expats, it wasn't long before word spread that I was Mr Fixit for anyone in a jam. And so it was that I got a call to help some Australians who were in a real mess with a couple of monkeys.

We all love monkeys, but from a vet's point of view they are a nightmare. Everyone is fascinated with them because they are versions of ourselves and can copy what humans do. Scratch your head and a monkey will scratch its. And then they'll do something crazy like suddenly leap and swing from limb to limb. People can't resist them. They'll even dress them up like little humans if they can.

Monkeys are smart. They've got opposing thumbs and fingers and that means they can do stuff. The little bastards are strong, too, and that's the problem. With their incredible grip they can open anything, pull anything and break anything more efficiently than humans can. From the point of view of a vet it actually makes them way more dangerous to deal with than lions or tigers.

If you wanted to indulge your fantasy of owning a monkey in the UAE it was easy: all you had to do was drop down to the local market, hand over your money and you could take one home. And that's exactly what had happened. Friends of friends had acquired a couple of cute little fellows from the market near Al Ain. Unfortunately, of course, the monkey doesn't come with an instruction manual, and now they were at their wits' end.

I arrived to find the couple had rented two apartments: one for them to live in, the other for the monkeys. They warned me that things had got somewhat out of control, and on opening the door I could see what they meant. I had some trepidation about this call, but the apartment was worse than I could have imagined. It was mayhem, like something out of the Gaza Strip. The monkeys had destroyed everything, and I mean *everything*. Fixtures had been pulled off the walls. Light fittings were twisted and smashed; it was amazing they hadn't munched through the wires and electrocuted themselves. Food was spread all over the place. They'd been shitting on the floor. It was just a disaster.

I could see pretty clearly what had happened. Monkeys are naturally inquisitive and like to investigate things, so if there's nothing for them to do they get bored. The couple told me they spent a fair bit of time with them but it's like a spoiled kid: you tell a kid it's time to go to bed but they keep wanting to watch television and make a fuss. Monkeys are the same. They want attention and, once they're bored, they start looking for stuff to do.

It was clear that there was a bit of a 'mum, dad and the kids' thing going on. The owners really had tried to anthropomorphise them, originally keeping the monkeys in a cage but then deciding that wasn't fair: the poor things should have more space. That worked fine for a while until the male got upset if they put too much pressure on him and tried to stop him doing what he wanted to do.

They weren't aggressive as such, but the couple wondered if I could give the monkeys some medication to be better behaved. Like Prozac, did they mean?

The problem was that, as cute as they are, you can never trust these things. As a student vet I'd witnessed a terrible incident at Melbourne zoo involving a gibbon called Charlie. Charlie was the darling of the crowds, a really cute little fellow. One day a keeper with very long hair got a bit too close to Charlie's cage and, quick as a flash, cute little Charlie grabbed the keeper's hair on both sides of his head and smashed his face against the bars right in front of me. The guy was knocked out cold in about a quarter of a second, on the ground and bleeding. The gibbon really beat the shit out of him. And Charlie thought that was pretty clever.

My advice to the couple was to just get rid of the monkeys. They were not going to win here. In the end, I think they surrendered them to a zoo.

And I doubt they got their bond back on the apartment.

■　■　■

The monkey episode was just a page in my growing portfolio of extracurricular activities. Some I did simply because I was the go-to guy for other western expats who I'd meet at a function, and later find myself on speed dial when things went wrong with their animal.

Some of my other activities, though, were very much linked to my new alter ego as Harry the Camel. It was all part of keeping myself so busy that I wouldn't have time to dwell on the loss of Natalia. In truth, the only problems I have ever had in the UAE have come from dealing with expats rather than the locals. And I was about to get my first dose of that.

Word had spread around the camel community back in Australia of the work we were doing in Al Ain. A couple of Australian hopefuls heard of the lucrative prize money on offer and thought they might as well have a crack at it, too. Bringing over a bunch of camels they had trained using treadmills in Australia, they put out the challenge that they were here to take on the best the UAE had to offer.

This was big news in Dubai, where Sheikh Mohammed bin Rashid Al Maktoum ran the largest and most successful camel operation in the world. In boxing terms, he was the undisputed world champion.

It came at a time when Dubai was redefining the whole idea of an Arab city, starting on the road to becoming a major business and tourist hub with some of the world's most outlandish attractions, like an indoor ski-field, where you could think you were in the Swiss Alps rather than a desert city with fifty-degree heat raging outside. Dubai was turning into the glitter capital of the Gulf.

The challenge was out and arrangements were made for the Australian camels to compete against Dubai's finest. Heath and I were curious to have a look at these blow-ins. We took ourselves off to the camp they'd set up in Dubai and coincidentally arrived at about the same time as Sheikh Mohammed, who had dropped in to check the quality of the title contenders. Being next in line as the Ruler of Dubai, Sheikh Mohammed was of course surrounded by tight security.

None of this bothered Heath, who has what you might call a healthy disdain for protocol. In fact, Heath didn't give a damn what your title was. He treated everyone exactly the same. Cutting through all the palaver, Heath started a discussion with Sheikh Mohammed, who, of course, was very interested to hear that we were from Abu Dhabi. Word had leaked out in the Gulf camel world that we were doing something with embryo transfer, though the details were not well known. Sheikh Mohammed took up the theme and told us that

Dubai would be the first to produce an embryo transfer calf. Most westerners in this situation would nod and politely agree, but not Heath. He was the opposite of the fawning, on-the-make westerner you so often find in the UAE; I loved him for it, and I suspect the royal families he dealt with might have felt the same. Heath laughed and told Sheikh Mohammed there was no way Dubai would be first: that would be us. Sheikh Mohammed smiled and wished us the best, no doubt certain Dubai would win out.

The great showdown was to be held the following day. Dubai's leading camel track was closed to the public and the Dubai royal family came out to watch. In the event, the Australian camels got absolutely hammered. The challenge was a grand flop and the swaggering Aussies were left to limp off into the sunset.

Suddenly, though, the Australians behind the scheme had two problems. They had spent a small fortune on their flight of fancy and now they had a dozen camels which they couldn't take back to Australia and that no-one in the UAE wanted. To top it off, a couple of Sheikh Mohammed's camels became sick and rumour spread that the Australian camels were the source, even though that was pretty well impossible given that Australian camels are disease-free.

The Aussie boys were in a fix so I rang them with an offer to take all twelve camels off their hands and keep them in a mate's camp. But now I had a problem: these things were expensive to feed and maintain, so I had to find a way to make money out of them. I had an idea: my old friend Paddy McHugh had turned a handy dollar offering camel rides into the outback, so why not try that here? Camel rides were big business in the tourist spots of Egypt and Jordan, but our research showed that, believe it or not, there were no camel ride businesses in the UAE. Indeed, there wasn't a single one in the entire Arabian Gulf.

Doug Cluer and I decided to be the first to set up camel safaris in the Gulf, as a private sideline to our work at the camel centre. This was no problem, as long as it didn't get in the way of our work for the Crown Prince. It started off small. Our initial customers were the US and Australian military personnel who had gathered in Al Ain for the first Iraq war mission, in the early nineties. We took groups a little way out into the desert for day trips and pegged out tents in an idyllic little oasis, where palm trees grew out of sand dunes and water flowed, just like the postcards. It was far enough away from the highway to feel that you were in the middle of nowhere, a welcoming island in a sea of sand. You could almost hear the strains of Maria Muldaur's 'Midnight at the Oasis'. The military guys also started bringing down their mates who were in Dubai on R and R, and this plus general word of mouth meant we became a little bit successful.

The camel safari business also spawned a very lucrative sideline. We started offering camel rides at the Fun City theme park in Al Ain, a magnet for expats and locals on the weekends. One of our innovations was to build a special ramp to walk up and take your position on top the camel, rather than going through the whole rigmarole of stopping the camel, have it sit down and get people to mount it on the ground. This worked like a charm because we could get the camels moving round and round in a super-efficient circle.

One of our customers turned out to be a sheikh in his early forties, and this was the first time he had ever ridden a camel. I told him he was going to find this a bit ironic: not only was it his first time on a camel, the camel was actually Australian, as were the blokes giving the riding lesson! It was a coals-to-Newcastle moment that neatly captured how citified and westernised some younger generation Emiratis had become.

The business was going gangbusters. At $1.50 a ride, it netted us a tidy few thousand dollars a week. But there was one snag: setting up a business in the UAE requires a local partner, so we still didn't have an official licence to operate. We just did it.

Technically, we were very open at this point to being prosecuted, thrown in gaol and/or deported. We desperately needed a local sponsor to be in business with us. An Emirati friend had the perfect solution: a man who was the former head of Interpol for the Middle East. As a senior security official in a country where security matters, our new connection, Juma, was supremely well connected. His dad had been born in an oasis near to Al Ain and was very close to the President of the UAE, Sheikh Zayed, and Juma had plenty of hand-me-down stories of the days when the tribes of Abu Dhabi fought against the tribes of Dubai in the 1960s.

Juma was tough as teak, a real camel man, and in his retirement he also dabbled in racing his own camels. He was keen to be involved as our business sponsor; this was good for us and good for him, too, because he instantly became the fifty-one per cent owner and therefore eligible for a large share of the profits.

What could be better? We had one thriving business in a beautiful oasis close to the camel research centre, another business an hour or so away in Dubai turning a very handy profit, and we were in cahoots with one of the UAE's most respected security chiefs.

Both ventures went from strength to strength. We built the herd up to twenty-five camels. We designed a brilliant new saddle in a classic Arabesque style with lovely soft sheepskins to provide comfort for western bottoms. Then we added some luxury touches to the basic experience, introducing the overnight safari where tourists got to stay in a gorgeous black goats hair Bedouin tent. Riding their camels through the desert, tourists had the illusion of being in the middle of nowhere, though in fact they were only five kilometres from the main road. As we served them Arabic coffee after a dinner catered by the Hilton Hotel, we had a fund of tall tales to tell tourists camped out around the fire.

Then we started getting very clever indeed, employing a couple of young British expats as managers and extending our camel ride business to other parts of the UAE, including the emirate of Sharjah. It was operating like a franchise. We had all the tour operators sewn up and if anyone wanted a camel ride, they had to come to us.

And then it suddenly unravelled. Badly.

Unbeknownst to us, our young British expat managers were double-dealing. They got in touch directly with Juma and convinced him that we were keeping the lion's share of the money. Perhaps it was their attempt to curry favour with Juma and get hold of the business for themselves. Needless to say, Juma didn't take well to the idea that we were ripping him off, even though it wasn't true. Things got ugly and Juma locked us out of the business immediately. We found we were seriously out of favour with a man who could now do us real damage.

There are many stories of expats coming unstuck in the UAE. Sometimes they hit the headlines, like the case of the Australian businessmen Marcus Lee and Matt Joyce, who were imprisoned for several years on accusations of fraud before being released. But for every one of those high-profile cases there are dozens of smaller cases you never hear about, where expats spend time in prison before being quietly released and deported after the diplomats get involved.

All these cases have one thing in common: life in the UAE was a bunch of roses until suddenly it all disintegrated. It was a fine line—sometimes an invisible line—between having it all and then watching it all go down the drain.

It was then that I did the stupidest thing of my time living in the UAE, a total rush of blood where I behaved as though I was in Australia and applied my own form of justice. It was almost a catastrophe.

Having put a great deal of effort into building up the camel business, I thought, bugger it, these are our camels, our saddles and our business. So we got a mate who was a former SAS officer and hatched a plan to get it all back.

The operation was planned meticulously. Doug and I, together with the old SAS man, would strike before dawn as everyone slept and make good our escape. So at five in the morning, commando-style, the three of us slipped silently into the camel camp, herded the camels together, scooped up our saddles and whatnot and made off with everything, lock, stock and barrel.

We were heading more or less calmly across the dunes and into the sunrise, feeling pleased with ourselves. The whole operation had gone off like clockwork. Just then there was the sound of sirens wailing from the direction of the camp. We had been busted, or so we thought. Now we started bolting across the dunes in a flat panic. How was this possible? It had been planned with military precision. Later we discovered that the guy who delivered water to the camp had used the siren on his truck to wake up the residents.

By now we had put a fair distance between us and the scene of the 'crime'. We crossed over the freeway with our booty of camels and assorted paraphernalia and walked the whole lot back to another camel camp that we considered safe. Mission accomplished.

I still shake my head when I think about it. We had stolen our camels off the former head of Interpol! Of course the problem was that, in our rush to get our business back, none of us had thought through the consequences. It wouldn't be long before Juma would get word and the trail would lead to me. He was, after all, a trained investigator, and this had all the hallmarks of an inside job. In reality there was nowhere to hide. Having had the rush of blood, I now agonised about the fallout.

I came to the conclusion that I had to roll the dice and go direct to our boss, Mr Zuhair. We met with the great negotiator that evening in the Hilton. I had a strong sense that if we were going to get out of this then we had to create an air of crisis. I gambled that if we had a chance to explain the case fully to Juma then we might be able to justify our actions. Maybe we could get away with it.

We were deep into the secret business of Emirati politics— and we were the outsiders. It could have gone any direction. In a close-knit, tribal society like the UAE, personal connections can matter much more than the letter of the law. That certainly applies to those who were born and bred here, and whose fathers might know the president on first-name terms. But how would it play out for a foreigner, even one who was employed by the Crown Prince?

It was threatening to get hugely complicated for everybody. Trust had been breached. Individual judgements on us as foreigners would come into play. After all, we had been given the highest honour of all when we were taken to meet the Crown Prince in person. What sort of message did this send about the judgement of the gatekeepers like Mr Zuhair himself? Reputations were on the line.

The following day we had a big sit-down in the Hilton boardroom. Juma was on one side of the table, us camel rustlers were on the other. Juma let it be known that he was furious and felt personally betrayed. For our side, we protested that we were innocent, victims of vindictive lies and that we, too, felt betrayed. Why wouldn't Juma believe us? After an hour of heated argument, the situation calmed. There would be a price to pay: we agreed on a settlement deal where Juma would buy the business from us. As a quid pro quo the matter would go no further. Juma set the terms so he got a good deal. But on the flipside, it hadn't gone to the authorities and all the pain that would have caused, including, very likely, being sent to prison. You could say it was a form of local justice.

There was a partly satisfying footnote to the story. A month later we saw a newspaper report that the two young British expats who'd shafted us had been thrown into prison for attempting to abscond from their sponsor. Juma had done his own checks, worked out the truth and had them arrested. This was the final vindication we needed, because their actions had come very close to leading us into disaster. The sad side to the story was that one of the young Brits was the daughter of friends of ours.

Juma was then able to use his influence to obtain a decree from the president to the effect that he was the only person permitted to run camel safaris in the emirate of Abu Dhabi.

The whole episode demonstrated that having the right personal connections mattered. There are two systems of justice: the traditional, tribal way and the official way, through police and courts. With a personal relationship there was always a chance that people would step back and work out a way to fix things. That's one of the things I love about this place: nothing's black and white and there is more than one road to go down. There was always another way, always the possibility of a deal that might save face and reputations.

Juma told us that what was done was done. 'We Arabs forget everything after three sunsets,' he said.

In truth I think it took a lot longer than that. But without a deal I would have been finished there and then.

Ten
Million dollar baby

I've been through thousands of camel births over the decades, but there's none to match the arrival of Sumha's Girl (or 'Bint Sumha' in Arabic). She was the first embryo transfer calf from the Crown Prince's herd.

Aylan Al Muheiri, who'd been with us on the trip out to Australia, called me early in the morning with the news that Sumha's Girl had been born overnight, which is the typical birthing time for a camel. Aylan was overjoyed. '*Namoos*,' he said, using the Arabic word for congratulations used especially for camel achievements. He wanted to see us out at the stables straightaway.

We'd known the day was close. A day or so before, Sumha's Girl's mother had gone quiet and taken herself off into a corner. The Pakistani camel handlers had separated her from the rest of the herd and stayed with her around the clock. It was as though they were guarding Fort Knox, which in a way they were.

Now it was official. I got hold of Heath and Doug and I drove up to the Hilton to collect Angus McKinnon to get a first glimpse of our lab baby. By the time we arrived the handlers had disinfected the umbilical cord, generally cleaned up and made sure Sumha's Girl was feeding from her mother, which is a vital early sign that the baby is on track.

She was a frail little thing and quite skinny, probably because, being an experimental baby, she was born later in the season than usual. In all other respects though she looked like a normal baby camel, with soft brown down and gangly legs, all unsteady as she took her first unfamiliar steps.

Within a couple of hours Sumha's Girl attempted her first frolic around the paddock, at first a short distance from her mother and then a little further away before returning to safety again. She kicked out her legs as a first, instinctive test of her ability to defend herself. She made bleating sounds, similar to a lamb, as she communicated for the first time with her mother. As a pack animal, camels are very social, so you will hear a lot of 'chatter' in a paddock of newborns. In the first weeks they are so curious and social that they will sidle up and nuzzle or nibble your ear.

So Sumha's Girl was doing what all baby camels do. The big difference, of course, was that Sumha's Girl had the genes of a champion. Her genetic mother, Sumha, was amongst the fastest females in the UAE, and Sumha's eggs had been fertilised by the Crown Prince's best male, Mileh Khabeer.

It gives some idea of the value of this breakthrough that, back then—more than twenty years ago—this baby super camel was worth one million dollars at birth. Today it would be multiples of that. No wonder the camel boys hadn't taken their eyes off her for a minute.

Actually, to me, every camel birth is something of a wonder. A baby camel is all neck and legs. As it emerges, it looks more like a spider; you wonder how it can get out. But camels are fantastic at giving birth. They have fewer birthing problems than any other species. Generally, you see the face and nose come out through the birth canal first, because of the long neck. Then you soon see the feet, and out it comes.

For all that, though, you never know until it happens. On this occasion we had taken a lot of precautions. All the surrogate mothers were being kept in a remote patch of desert owned by the Crown Prince. This was a secret operation, so access was heavily restricted. Here they had an outdoor paddock to themselves. We'd built stables for each of the surrogates, so they could be kept inside and protected from the elements. In March it can be cold, especially at night, and you get a bit of rain and wind, which isn't good for any animal about to give birth.

In the days after Sumha's Girl there were five more live calves from different surrogate mothers, all a result of the union of Sumha and Mileh Khabeer. This represented twelve years of Sumha's breeding potential, produced in just one season. We had in fact produced twelve fertilised eggs from Sumha that we transferred to twelve surrogates. Out of those, six camels became pregnant.

The birth of Sumha's Girl was the culmination of more than eighteen months of dreams, plans and sheer hard work. Seeing her for the first time, I felt a combination of excitement and massive relief. It was absolutely fantastic. Heath Harris was beaming, as though he was the actual father, which in a way he was after making his wild promises to the royal family. His was in every sense a triumph of optimism over experience.

For me it was a hugely emotional moment—the end of a long hard road from the time Heath stuck his neck out and said he would deliver on something that had never been done before. We had travelled to Western Australia. Patti and I had lost Natalia. And here we had achieved a world first. The amount of time and effort that had gone into this moment was astronomical. There were about thirty steps in getting to this point and there were so many places where it could have all gone wrong. But it hadn't.

There was much riding on the success of the first embryo transfer, from the very top of the UAE down. In fact, there was way more interest than even we had suspected at the time. We knew that the president had taken time out from a state visit to Japan to call about our progress, but we also later learned that the Crown Prince would occasionally be driven up to the camel camp and spend the early evening sitting in the sand with the first batch of embryo transfer camels, before quietly slipping away back to his palace.

Once we'd started the embryo transfer with the Crown Prince's camels, there was a huge amount of anticipation. From day one Mr Zuhair would constantly be dropping down to the lab to inquire if we had a pregnancy yet. It was fortunate that we were able to produce results quickly, though it can never be quickly enough when someone wants a result yesterday.

Aylan Al Muheiri had been given direct responsibility for the reproductive project and was very hands-on. He too was always in the lab, asking questions about where we were up to. As he squinted down the microscope, it was very hard to convince him that that little ball he could see floating in fluid was really a baby camel seven days after conception that would one day be a calf.

You could see how excited Aylan was as he ran around the paddock like a little kid in the first week with these babies. He knew they were special. And he too was relieved because he had good news to report up the line.

The six live births had been hugely helpful for our relationship with the trainers and camel handlers. Just eighteen months before, the only treatments they had been using were those handed down unchanged over hundreds of years. Now suddenly they had to accept the idea that you could put together the eggs and the semen of two animals, extract the embryo and impregnate a third camel to carry the baby to birth.

Then there was the added dimension that the surrogate mothers weren't the slim, brown racing camels they knew. Halfway through the program, the Crown Prince had decided that the surrogates should be a different breed altogether. Sheikh

Khalifa wanted to use huge black camels called Hazmis, which were typically used in Saudi Arabia as milk camels. He judged that they would be better recipients because they were bigger, had more room in the uterus and a better milk supply.

It was virtually impossible to explain to the Bedouin how all this could work, even though there is no physiological difference between these two breeds when it comes to reproduction. They simply had to take it on trust that a fine brown racing camel baby would emerge from a hulking black milk camel, with some very fancy lab work in between. There was a lot on the line.

It was a major stroke of luck that not only were the calves born healthy but that four of the six were female, since females are superior when it comes to speed. If we'd had five males and one female, there's no doubt it would have made it harder to convince the locals of the value of our work.

In scientific terms, so much was unique in what we had done. We had broken new ground every step of the way and done it without the benefit of a body of science to guide us. We would learn more later. For one thing, the camel is different to most other animals because the very act of mating helps stimulate the release of an egg. This means that simply fertilising an egg through artificial insemination won't give the best result.

We celebrated the moment very well that night at the hotel, but in truth the magnitude of what we had achieved only really hit home when I later saw coverage of it on the front page of *The Age* newspaper in Melbourne. Such was the reluctance of the Crown Prince's men to publicise the achievement that the story only saw the light of day two and a half years after the event and was written up as a feel-good Christmas piece.

Riding the local angle for all it was worth, the paper carried a report headlined 'Australian vets perfect world's first camel embryo transfer'. The first paragraph said: 'Take three wise men, a desert landscape and a camel named Sumha and you have a science Christmas story.' Two of the 'three wise men' were

Dr Angus McKinnon of the University of Melbourne and myself; the third was the Crown Prince. It was an amusing mash-up of the Christian birth story in Bethlehem, which happened to be thousands of kilometres away. The Muslim Crown Prince might also have been somewhat bemused to find himself lumped in with a Christian trio. Nevertheless, it captured the idea of a miracle birth, even if science was the father.

It was only then, seeing it in print, that I fully comprehended how big the achievement was. Our world first was really something extraordinary, not just for the camel world but for veterinary science.

■ ■ ■

We were finally on our way to making the Crown Prince's camels the best in the Gulf and, though there was still a way to go, we now had a tool in our armoury that left our opponents flat-footed.

Mr Zuhair was well pleased. He had informed the Crown Prince and His Highness was delighted. It meant enormous kudos not just for the centre built in his name but also for his father, the president, and for the emirate of Abu Dhabi. It justified the investment he'd put into getting western experts like us over to Al Ain to set up the centre as a truly pioneering institution.

On the strength of the breakthrough, Sheikh Khalifa ordered that a further ten million dollars be spent on establishing a special centre for researching reproductive physiology and breeding superior racing camels. Our small research centre was now to be transformed into a major new Gulf institution, which became known as the Hilli Embryo Transfer Centre for Racing Camels.

This, too, was all top-secret. The centre needed to be constructed somewhere remote. A site had been found in the area of Hilli a few kilometres north of Al Ain, hidden behind sand dunes and accessible only by a compacted-sand track. Security barriers would be erected to stop any unauthorised access.

The aim was to make the Hilli centre a veritable breeding factory for racing camels. Retired racing camels with superior pedigree and performance would be identified and sent there for breeding, using embryo transfer technology. The complex would include a huge new lab, with advanced reproductive equipment sourced from all over the world. There would be an indoor handling facility, which would allow us to keep the camel immobile while we conducted ultrasonic examinations and collected and transferred embryos. The staff would swell from ten to thirty or more, including camel handlers. With air-conditioning it would be possible to work through the heat of the summer months and keep research projects on the go all year round. This would add another five months and effectively double the time we had at our disposal to produce more embryo camels.

We'd had a fifty per cent success rate for our first attempt with the Crown Prince's racing camels, so we knew there was scope to improve our techniques further. Immediately we would be able to refine our methods and push up pregnancy rates to make them comparable with other domestic species, where the success rate was as high as sixty-five to seventy per cent.

As good as it was, embryo transfer was just the tip of the iceberg. Now that we had established that you could produce multiple embryos from a camel, all other reproductive techniques were open to us. Our next aim was to produce camel calves from frozen embryos. This would allow us to freeze any embryos we were unable to transfer immediately, giving us much greater flexibility. And there were other techniques to be explored, such as semen freezing, artificial insemination and in-vitro fertilisation. Each and every one of these would give us another way to maximise the genes of our best camels.

Yet with all our progress, we were still walking on eggshells, pardon the pun. Not everyone was pleased with the progress we had made. In bringing the latest fruits of modern science to bear, we were tampering with an animal that is *the* symbol of ancient Arabia. Here, literally, was the collision point of science, culture and faith. The developments posed a further threat to some of the established trainers, many of whom were already leery of even conventional procedures such as injections. They feared that our breeding techniques would essentially make them redundant. After all, who needs a trainer to work their secret magic when you have genetically superior camels being turned out of a lab?

It was no small concern. There are vast amounts of money washing around the camel races, and trainers are the chief beneficiaries. Indeed, the best of the trainers might earn well over a million dollars a year from their share of the prize money given at the huge number of races that are held, with cash prizes all the way down to tenth place. The trainers, in turn, would use these funds to provide for their families and some of their tribe. Thus the trainers played a key role in an informal social security and reward system that redistributed petro-dollars and contributed enormously to the stability of their society.

So the revolutionary techniques we introduced had the potential to become a serious social issue, well beyond just making a faster camel. Eventually this, more than any other factor, would work against us.

■ ■ ■

You might imagine that there would have been a huge hulla-balloo surrounding the birth of Sumha's Girl. But there wasn't. She was certainly an instant celebrity for the select few who witnessed her first steps that day. However, as significant as our achievement was, we were under orders not to disclose details of the science that lay behind it. The technology we used was a secret, and in the arms race to develop the fastest camels, we were in the equivalent of Los Alamos.

Heath Harris would have a bit of fun with all the secrecy. When visitors were due from Dubai, he would leave out files marked 'Top-secret: The Speed Gene' for a bit of a lark. Who knows what tall tales returned about what was really going on in Al Ain.

It was a year after the birth before we were permitted to present our work publicly for the first time. This was to a scientific gathering at the world's first camel conference, held in Dubai.

Like all things Dubai, this was a grand and sumptuous occasion, bringing together the best of international knowl-edge. There were experts from Canada, the United States, the United Kingdom and North Africa. Most were very well known for their work with horses, which they had adapted to camels. Nearly all of them worked for the various Gulf royal families trying to make their camels the best.

The most advanced research work up to this point had been done in Dubai. Sheikh Mohammed bin Rashid Al Maktoum had assembled a formidable research team headed by fertil-ity experts and microbiologists drawn from the Newmarket stables in the United Kingdom, generally considered to be the global centre of thoroughbred horseracing. It was also the UK headquarters for training Sheikh Mohammed's horses.

The leading light from Newmarket was Professor William 'Twink' Allen, who was renowned in the horse world for his work running the equine fertility unit at Robinson College in Cambridge and then Newmarket. Twink's daughter ultimately married Sheikh Mohammed's chief jockey, Frankie Dettori. Both Twink and English scientist Lulu Skidmore had been recruited to work with Sheikh Mohammed's racing camels.

The contest between Dubai and Abu Dhabi was therefore very much England versus Australia, with Angus McKinnon, Doug Cluer and I working for Abu Dhabi.

At the camel conference, the Dubai team gave an impressive presentation on their research on superovulation, showing how they were able to detect follicles in the uterus at various stages of development. If Dubai was superovulating camels then clearly, for all our secrecy, word had leaked out beyond our little group that we had been working on embryo transfer. Either that or Dubai's experts had independently taken the same approach as Heath had: give it a go and see what happens.

When it came to our turn, we were able to report the results of 121 embryo transfers leading to thirty-five pregnancies. We had already produced results while Dubai was still in the research stage. I was also able to present a paper on the pioneering use of ultrasound to monitor the reproductive cycle of the camel. It was apparent that we had been more practical in our work and that we saw the bigger picture of where all this could go.

We were one up on our rivals that day. But in the battle unfolding for camel supremacy, the Abu Dhabi–Australia team still had a long way to go.

Eleven
When Katya met Khaled

The early success of the embryo transfer program banished any thoughts of us being packed off back to Australia.

Along the way I learned a valuable lesson. The sheikhs who run the country certainly want to see results for their money, but at the same time they were capable of being far more tolerant of failure than people in western society. They took the view that, no matter how much you planned for things to happen, in the end whatever comes to pass is God's will.

This belief permeates every aspect of life and in some ways it makes for a far more relaxed approach to getting things done. Why sweat it if it's beyond your control? It's a liberating thought if you can embrace it, and a helpful attitude in a country that in so many ways was a giant start-up. Some things work, some things don't. If you set off with a fear of failure, you get nowhere.

I liked that spirit and I liked the place; it gave me a sense of freedom that I could never feel in Australia. Bit by bit, we had put down roots. Al Ain felt like home. Subconsciously,

I might even have begun to feel that it was a place I might never leave.

After five years, I was the only one left standing from the original gang that had come over to set up the camel centre. Geoff Manefield had been the first to depart, followed by Heath, who returned full-time to training horses. Everyone wanted Heath for his ability to make a horse do whatever needed to be done; if you wanted a horse to dance a jig, Heath was your man. He had no shortage of offers to work on major movies and television series all over the world. Doug Cluer was the last to call it quits. He and his family had headed back to Tweed Heads to pick up where they'd left off.

Even Mr Zuhair was leaving the project. It was really sad to lose him, but he was replaced by a member of the royal family who was very hands-on with the camels and wanted to drive our work forward. Sheikh Sultan was a cousin of the Crown Prince and also a personal adviser to him. He was a good judge of a camel and became very involved in deciding what animals we would buy.

This kind of turnover is par for the course in the UAE. The average lifecycle for an expat was, and remains, three to four years. For most people that's enough time on a generous tax-free salary and good working conditions to give them a pot of money to get on with. Mostly they want to get back home for the sake of their kids' education or to give them a sense of home.

For my part, though, I had no desire to go anywhere. The longer I stayed, the more I liked it. Patti was never one to turn her back on adventure either.

There are expats who just can't take the way of living and working in the UAE. It's a place where things don't always go according to plan. Projects can be delayed for no clear reason, or change course abruptly. Things don't always function like clockwork, as they might back home.

But for me, that's what made it so good. There were echoes of my early days back at the Bacchus Marsh Lion Safari Park, a large element of chaos that I loved. Is there anything more dull than predictability?

I realised early on that language was going to be key to both my long-term survival and ultimate success. I was dealing day-to-day with Emiratis and other Gulf Arabs who were born and raised in the desert. They were men who knew the business of camels and survival and who might barely have seen the inside of a classroom. So I set about acquiring their language, which is a particular form of Arabic, different to the standard Arabic that prevails across the Middle East. You won't find it in a textbook. The only way you can learn it is by constant interaction. The more I was able to converse with the Bedouin trainers, the more we understood what each of us had to offer and the more our respect for each other grew.

This was another universe, entirely different to what most western expats experience. English alone is fine if you are working in Dubai or Abu Dhabi. And, given that it is the international language of business, most younger Emiratis are being educated in English. Many are sent to schools in the UK or the USA, specifically to help them become fluent and able to negotiate with international partners. Al Ain was more traditional and conservative.

With us staying on, our daughters Katya and Erica were also saying goodbye to other expat kids and, in turn, making more and more friendships with the local kids. And that's how it all began for Katya and an Emirati boy called Khaled.

The international school that Katya went to was a melting pot for dozens of different cultures. There were the kids of American expats, British expats, Indian expats and Lebanese expats. There was even the hard-case son of a reputed Palestinian political heavyweight who'd been temporarily banished from Gaza, or so the gossip had it. Some Emirati families also sent their kids there to be educated in English.

Out of this mix, Katya and Khaled were drawn to each

other. Katya was fourteen and Khaled fifteen when their mutual crush developed.

Khaled was a great kid. Early on he turned up to our house with a snake that needed help, so he was immediately in my good books. Khaled had picked up a saw-scaled viper, which is not one of the deadliest snakes in the world but it still kills more people than just about every other snake.

These little vipers are all through North Africa and the Middle East. Normally they will sit in the sand and mind their own business—unless you happen to stand next to one, and then it will bite you. More often than not, this will happen to people in the middle of nowhere and they die simply because they can't get treatment.

There was a local custom where the boys would go into the desert and catch one of these saw-scaled vipers, stitch its mouth together with cotton thread and keep it in their pocket. Then, for a laugh, they would throw the viper at people and scare the shit out of them.

Khaled didn't want to play that game. He had rescued one of these poor creatures and brought it to me to remove the thread from its mouth, which I did very carefully, using a fine scalpel. It was then ready to be returned to the wild. Needless to say, Khaled won a lot of points with me for that.

It was only later on that Patti and I learned that Katya and Khaled had got themselves into trouble for holding hands at school. This might sound like the sort of low-level, innocent stuff that teenagers do but, even at this early stage, Katya and Khaled were breaking one of the unwritten rules which govern relations between expats and their Emirati hosts: by all means be good mates, but no more.

Actually it was a huge red line they were crossing, because Katya and Khaled were seeing each other outside of school as well. Khaled would turn up at odd hours and knock on the door to say hello to Katya, or he'd be over to watch Katya working with her horse.

For the first year or two we knew Katya and Khaled were keen on each other, but after a while we became concerned that this might be getting a little more serious than we had counted on. It was a dilemma that most western families in the UAE don't need to confront, simply because they live in isolation from the Emiratis. If we were crossing a threshold, we didn't know what the implications could be.

I had no problem in principle with Katya being keen on a local. In some ways it showed her willingness to be open to other influences, a trait Katya had seen at home and which had been instilled in me by my dad. On another level, though, it just didn't seem wise for Katya to become involved with someone and then have to leave; we didn't have any plans to go, but you never knew. The last thing we needed was any sort of trouble with a local family. And this wasn't just any family.

Khaled's family, the Mazroueis, are desert people through and through and have played a prominent part in the UAE's history. The Mazroueis have close ties with the Al Nahyan family that rules Abu Dhabi and the UAE. Khaled's grandfather is a revered figure in local lore: the UAE president called him the 'Emir', an affectionate term loosely meaning 'he who must be obeyed'.

It is a measure of the family's standing that a Mazrouei woman is married to my ultimate boss, Sheikh Khalifa, then the Crown Prince and now President of the United Arab Emirates. In the natural course of events, the Mazroueis might expect that Khaled too might marry into the ruling family. At the very least he would marry into another leading local family or tribe.

We knew this was going to be difficult to navigate. There were a host of cultural issues to take into account. In short, a Mazrouei being with a western girl could get complicated. I sought the counsel of an old Emirati friend, Mohammed Al Dhaheri, on the best way to navigate this minefield. Mohammed was of the view that a meeting needed to be brokered between the families to gently tease out the awkward situation. His advice was that this would be best handled by the mothers, who arranged to meet.

As a sign of respect for her standing in their society, Khaled's mother, Fatima, was known as Sheikha Fatima—'Sheikha' is the term for the wife of the leader of a tribe. Fatima was from the generation of Emirati women who would only ever appear in public fully covered, including a veil over her face with a narrow slit where her eyes were visible. So it would have been easy to assume she could be a little hostile.

As it turned out, there was nothing forbidding or fearsome at all about Fatima. She welcomed Patti into her family home. Khaled's mother, it turned out, had held the same suspicions and fears as us. The two women compared notes and agreed that, yes, Katya and Khaled were too young and they needed to be kept apart. Thankfully, she held no animosity towards us whatsoever, even though our daughter might have been judged to have turned her son away from the right path for an Emirati boy.

We decided that the solution was to send Katya to boarding school back in Melbourne. We had family there who could look after her. And besides, we needed to make sure Katya had the best possible education for her last two years of school.

Before sending her back to Australia I invited Khaled to meet for coffee at the Hilton Hotel, scene of many a delicate negotiation. I told him he and Katya were too young and that they needed to concentrate on their studies. And I pointed out that Fatima was of the same mind. Khaled looked at me and agreed.

I spoke to Katya separately and gave her the same message. She also looked at me and agreed. Reluctantly. She was none too happy about it.

But I'm sure they both knew this wasn't the end of the story. Not by a long way. There was an ember burning and it might not be easy to snuff this one out.

Twelve
Camel vet to desert vet

As the vet in charge of a reproductive program, I would spend half my waking hours with my right arm shoved up the rear of a camel. It's not everyone's cup of tea, but that's what goes with the territory when you're breeding the world's fastest racing camels.

Everything happens at the rear of a camel. You reach deep inside the rectum with a small ultrasonic probe to get the best view of how many eggs a female is producing. When it comes to getting the embryos out, a large bagful of fluid is squeezed in through the rear to flush the embryos out into a collection tube. From there it's off to a microscope to examine the quality of the embryos, but then it's back to the rear again to implant an embryo into the uterus of a surrogate.

This is a cycle I came to repeat thousands of times. The Hilli Embryo Transfer Centre for Racing Camels was beautifully set up to make it all happen with a minimum of fuss or wasted time. We refined every step in the process to make it incredibly efficient.

Traditionally, to treat a camel it needs to fold its legs and sit on the ground, but we devised a method of treating a camel standing up. We used a cattle crush chute to contain them, with bars under the belly of the camel and, to keep it still, bars across its chest and rear. This allowed us to push each camel through in about a minute, compared with the twenty or so minutes it takes to treat a camel sitting down. With three crushes erected side by side, I could move from one to the other while more camels were led in to take their place.

Over the years, Hilli turned out thousands of embryos and hundreds of successful births. It was all ticking over like a machine. Examine, ultrasound, flush, implant. Examine, ultrasound, flush, implant.

It might sound like a factory, but this did not take away the delight I felt every time a baby camel came into the world. I got a special thrill knowing that I had flushed it as an eight-day embryo from its mother, and washed and handled it as a microscopic being. The many stages were recorded and dated by hand and kept in large ring-bound folders on my bookcase. I know it's not the traditional baby book, but there were massive amounts of devotion and care poured into each birth.

■ ■ ■

With my credentials as the camel vet well established, I found my services being called on to tend to the sheikhs' other creatures. The call always came out of the blue and it always sent my day sideways. But if it took me away from the rear of a camel for a while, I wasn't complaining.

This, of course, was not strictly in my brief. I was hired to be the camel vet but, as I was becoming aware, an employment contract was not much more than a rough guide. Being employed by sheikhs can mean you are pretty much on call for anything. In fact, you never quite knew what would come next.

Apart from that, a regional town like Al Ain meant a close-knit community where things were done on a very personal level. If you were the best qualified then of course you should help out, even if you're not strictly an expert.

Thus I found I was morphing, gradually, from the camel vet to the desert vet.

My new boss, Sheikh Sultan, was very hands-on with the camels, but he also had a vast private zoo at his farm. This was where he went to relax, and it was something of a fantasy land. Apart from the animals, the farm was also home to his private collection of two dozen of the world's rarest and most valuable cars, all limited-edition, exclusive marques such as the Bugatti Veyron, the fastest street-legal production car in the world. There was a set of Ferraris—from the antique to the latest concept cars—and the gull-winged Mercedes, produced in 1959 and acquired from the Mercedes-Benz Museum in Stuttgart. The collection was kept in a large display area inside a complex that included a swimming pool, a bowling lane and an elevated private office, from which the sheikh could survey his collection.

The sheikh's farm was hidden from public view by a high concrete and brick fence which ran, it seemed, for kilometres. Driving in was like entering a whole new landscape, the desert transformed into something more like a forest, with date palms, hundreds of trees and lots of vegetation. To achieve this in the desert is quite an engineering feat, involving laying massive pipes to bring water to the property and then an intricate watering system.

The sheikh had a section for the camels and a separate area for the horses, plus a small enclosure for goats and sheep, which were likely to provide a feast for any visitor. He also kept a huge herd of around two thousand Arabian gazelles plus a small number of cheetahs over the years. But the centrepiece—and what made the sheikh's farm special—was a closed-off area of around ten hectares set aside for his collection of Arabian oryx.

Next to the camel, the oryx is my favourite desert animal. It has the bearing of the antelope you find in Africa, but it is much slimmer. Its horns are very straight so, when you look at it side-on, it appears to have a long single horn coming out of its head, which is why the oryx is said to have inspired the legend of the unicorn. The people of the desert might have relied on the camel for survival, but they considered the oryx to be a more beautiful, majestic animal. Some scientists also believe the oryx is even better adapted to the desert than the camel, which is a big claim, though they are certainly capable of surviving without water for very long periods. They are striking beasts in every way, which is no doubt why the animal has been adopted as a symbol throughout the Arabian Peninsula; it is the national animal of Oman and the symbol for Qatar Airways.

If you go to a zoo, you might see one or two oryx. The sheikh had about fifty of them roaming free. It was exhilarating to see them in such numbers.

Even if it was something relatively minor, like stitching a cut or taking blood, there was no such thing as an easy job when dealing with these animals. The oryx's horns are long and sharp, and they use them to impale their prey. That makes working with them really dangerous.

First I needed to corral the oryx into a holding pen in the centre of the farm. The idea was to run them into a funnel that led them down into a confined area. Once the oryx was trapped, three or four farm workers would lean over the wooden barrier and grab onto its horns, to prevent it from swinging its head around to gore me.

Everything needed to be done rapid-fire. A restrained wild animal is stressed, and the workers are holding on for dear life. There's adrenalin everywhere. So I had to move fast.

First step was to jab in a syringe to take blood, but there was no time to wait around for the result. So I had to take a punt on what the problem was and maybe try a long-acting shot of antibiotic, something to last four or five days. Or perhaps an antipyretic to reduce a fever, hoping that whatever they have isn't too serious. Once results of the blood tests are in I could follow up with an oral treatment, assuming the animal gets back on their food or is at least drinking water.

Ideally the whole operation is over in just a couple of minutes, which is more than long enough for those workers hanging onto those killer horns. But you need to make it count because nobody wants to be in the position of trying to catch the animal a second time. The first time, okay, you might catch it by surprise. After that they get to know the routine. They're not so stupid that they'll fall for the old funnel trick again, plus if you chase an oryx for more than five minutes and put them under stress, they are vulnerable to a syndrome called capture myopathy, which means they have so much adrenalin coursing through them—due to the fight or flight mechanism—that their muscles break down and they drop dead. It's a common reaction in wild animals. Predators in the wild normally move in for the kill very quickly and it's usually all over in two minutes, so their prey are simply not physiologically equipped for long chases.

This means you have to be very methodical when you capture an animal like an oryx. Chasing them around and around until they get exhausted isn't an option and is especially bad when they're being chased in confinement. The animals also get more resistant to the knockout drugs you are using and you end up needing bigger and bigger doses to get the same effect.

It's always such a drama.

■　■　■

The sheikhs have a special affinity not only with camels but with wildlife in general. They love owning exotic animals and just about every sheikh has his own private zoo. Unlike most of us, they have the wealth to assemble their collections from all over the world. Going to these zoos means you enter the private world of the sheikhs, a world foreigners rarely get to glimpse. Some sheikhs have a particular fascination for the big cats of Africa: the lions, tigers and cheetahs. Others have everything.

One of my common call-outs was to the Crown Prince's son, whose palace was just down the road from my house in Al Ain. He had a huge wildlife collection, including animals native to the Arabian Gulf such as the oryx, the ibex and the gazelle, as well as others like wolves, tigers and lions. You name it, he had it. Typically I would go there to advise on feeding and how to control parasites.

My ultimate boss, Sheikh Khalifa, had created a landscape of rolling green hills by growing grass on ten hectares of sand dunes inside his Al Ain palace to create lush fields where the sheikh's collection of oryx could run and graze freely. The Crown Prince had also created a research area inside his palace for breeding endangered species of the Arabian Peninsula, with separate pens for the straight-horned Arabian oryx and its cousin the scimitar oryx, with its long, curved horns, as well as the Arabian tahr, one of his favourites.

Most of my jobs were straightforward distress calls for various misadventures. For example, a leopard might have become caught in a fence and needed to be pacified to release it. The wolves were particularly problematic: put two of them together and, sure as eggs, they'll take a piece out of each other and you need to stitch them up. I always kept a full veterinary medical kit in the back of my four-wheel drive, along with a fridge containing antibiotics and other medicines. When I had to attend to an injured wolf I always threw in an extra supply of sutures and needles.

Courtesy of my time as a graduate vet at the Lion Safari Park in Bacchus Marsh, I already had experience with the big cats. But the first time I dealt with a wolf was at Sheikh Sultan's farm.

I arrived to find a timber wolf pacing up and down in a small open enclosure. It had picked up some serious gashes to its legs after a fight with another wolf and by now was quite agitated. It wasn't life-threatening, but every case has its own demands. I was surprised by the size of the timber wolf. It's a big rangy animal, but also very thin.

With a timber wolf as much as an oryx, you need to sum up the situation quickly and then move. A timber wolf is like a dog, but if anything it is smarter and more attuned to survival. An animal can smell fear, but it can also pick up on indecision. So, as a vet, it is essential to be authoritative around an animal.

The sheikh's animal handlers had managed to separate the wolves, but beyond that they had no idea of what to do. You might be able to approach an injured dog, but a wild wolf was another matter. First I needed to get the injured animal into a smaller fenced-off area. Once it was there, I jabbed a needle through the wire to knock it out. When it was tranquillised we dragged the animal out onto open ground, clipped off the fur around the injured areas, cleaned the wounds and got to work with the stitching. Then I injected a long-acting antibiotic.

I was always happy to work on cheetahs. I have seen a few of them over the years, for everything from a simple vaccination to fixing a broken leg. Cheetahs are classified as cats, but in reality they are much more doglike. Unlike all the other big cats, the cheetah's claws are semi-retractable, one of the anatomical adaptations that has made the cheetah the fastest land animal in the world. But though it is a prolific hunter in the wild, it is relatively easy to domesticate, which is why they are a pet of choice for sheikhs in the UAE. Indeed there were plenty of stories of young sheikhs turning up to a café or some such with a cheetah on a lead, a little like a fashion accessory.

There's no way I would trust any other big cat. It would rip your head off.

A good Emirati friend of mine named Salim called me for a favour one day. One of his three pet cheetahs was limping badly so would I come out to take a look? I arrived to find this beautiful cat in real pain and barely able to lift its paw. Salim held on to it as I ran my hand around its lower leg. I could feel that one of the two main bones in its leg, the ulna, was fractured. The radius bone was intact.

The animal was so tame Salim was able to hold it against his legs while I administered the tranquilliser. From there it was a matter of applying a plaster cast to immobilise the leg for several weeks.

This close relationship with animals is something I love about life in the UAE. It resonates with me, not only as a vet but as a human being. There are simply fewer barriers between humans and animals. In western countries like Australia, people are alienated from animals. There are rules for this and rules for that. Yes, you have to be sure that animal welfare is being looked after and that animals aren't endangered, but in Australia these days a kid can't even have a snake without a licence. Life is a lot poorer for that.

Thirteen
Leading by a nose

Sheikh Sultan was on the mobile and he was excited. Make that beside himself with happiness. 'Congratulations, congratulations!' The words were tumbling out. 'It was unbelievable. She ran like a horse!'

One of our camels, a female called Masah, had won a race where it counted: at a major event in Abu Dhabi for camels owned by UAE sheikhs. What made it so sweet was that Masah was one of our embryo camels.

I had no idea that one of our lab babies was even racing that day; this was something the sheikh kept to himself. He was well aware of the secretiveness that still surrounded the whole reproductive program and it was his policy to tell no-one, me included, if an embryo camel was racing. Indeed the trainers themselves had no idea if they were working with embryo camels or normal camels. The camels were all allocated by ballot to the trainers, with nothing to identify one from the other. The sheikh didn't want the Bedouin to know because he didn't want the embryo babies to be treated more or less preferentially than any other camel. It was entirely possible that the Bedouin trainers might have wanted to make them look bad.

Masah's win was our greatest triumph to date. I had been stuck doing something else and felt rotten for missing the moment, but I looked at the footage later and it was true. The race was run over six kilometres and Masah was well back in the pack with just 500 metres to go. Then she just took off and ran over the competition. She was one of our best, but in this race it was as though Masah was powered by a rocket, catching up and overtaking the leaders in no time flat. Masah had indeed 'run like a horse'. These were the sweetest words I could hear, and really it was the moment I had been working towards.

It wasn't yet a win at the very highest level, but Masah had proven that the Crown Prince now had a camel that was at least the equal of any Dubai camel. She went on to win a further seven races in a row.

Until Masah's win, the Crown Prince's camels were still running at their natural gait, which is more akin to a pacer in horse terms. They rarely, if ever, galloped. The difference is that a horse is designed to race, while a camel is not. A camel is knock-kneed, and on its rear legs its knees are at the back rather than the front of the leg. This makes it great at collapsing its legs under itself to sit in the desert, but the arrangement is not so great for running. The camel is like a diesel engine: turn it on and it goes forever. The horse is more like a petrol-powered V8, explosive and fast.

By nature, too, the camel doesn't do things at speed when left to its own devices. I love the fact that they are possessed with an incredible arrogance and self-confidence. They are a very relaxed animal and nothing fazes them. So it's not that they can't run fast, it's just that by and large they don't want to.

For our purposes it meant there was so much potential to improve the racing speed of the camel. Fortunately camel racing was, and remains, different to thoroughbred horseracing: there is no governing club that lays down the rules. Horseracing is still bound by old rules, which prevent high-tech reproductive manipulations such as artificial insemination, embryo transfer, IVF or cloning. That's one reason there has been very little change in the speed of horse races for decades. Winning times have barely shifted since the 1970s.

Not so in the world of camel racing. By the time Masah galloped we had already improved the speed of a camel by ten to fifteen per cent in the space of just six years. The competition with Dubai meant there was a camel arms race between the two city-emirates, with vast resources to play with and no limits on what could be done. Camel racing was becoming way more sophisticated than horseracing.

Of course, there was no manual around on how to increase the speed of a racing camel and improve its stamina. We were literally writing the book as we went. Around the time of Masah's win we were on the brink of producing another world first: the first camel calf from a frozen embryo, which would allow us to store embryos and use them at a time of our choosing. We kicked off early DNA research, and we set up a department to look at the types of bacteria, viruses and fungi that cause infections and lower performance. The treadmill research was yielding valuable data on the camel's heart rate and lactic acid levels under stress. All this allowed us to see how different medicines, feed and supplements affected performance. We discovered the importance of getting vitamin levels right, especially vitamins B1 and E.

At the same time, Dubai was hardly standing still. Sheikh Mohammed, then the Crown Prince, established the Godolphin horse stables, a monolithic racing and breeding operation. He was also creating a worldwide network of the best horse stables in the UK, the USA, Australia and Ireland and had assembled a great management team. In short, he was creating the largest and most expensive stable of fast horses in human history. All of this provided synergies with his extensive camel operation.

Sheikh Mohammed's profile meant that anyone in the world with half an idea that might improve the pace of a camel would get in touch with his operation: anything to enter the glittering kingdom that Dubai was becoming.

Dubai was investing major sums of money in reproduction technologies. It was even playing with different species and had produced the world's first 'cama' by crossing a camel with a llama, which is genetically linked to the camel family. It was working on crossing a two-hump camel with a one-hump camel and had had some success producing a faster breed.

Dubai was putting a huge focus on research, but I believed we were on the right track. By the time of Masah's win we had achieved so much, yet still the major prizes eluded us. We were at a critical juncture in the superheated competition with Dubai. Our masters, too, had a sense that this was the case.

For the first time I was summoned to meet personally with the Crown Prince. Unusually, there would be no entourage. This would not be part of a larger gathering.

Angus McKinnon and I arrived at Sheikh Khalifa's private palace in the capital, Abu Dhabi. There we were presented to the Crown Prince and his half-brother, Sheikh Mohammed bin Zayed, the next in line as Crown Prince of Abu Dhabi. I knew we had been summoned for good reasons, to talk about the reproduction program. The meeting lasted an hour and a half, which is a large chunk out of Sheikh Khalifa's diary. The mood was relaxed and jovial, but there was a serious edge. It might be too much to say it was a council of war, but the Crown Prince wanted to know from us if we had all the support and equipment we needed.

The whole racing game was changing and I had a sense now that we were out there in the front, leading it.

■ ■ ■

Through the 1990s the camel racing business leapt to a new level. The sport of sheikhs had become the growth industry of the Gulf.

In the UAE over a dozen new racetracks were built and old tracks revamped. There were around 35,000 racing camels in the UAE alone. It was attracting bigger and bigger turnouts from the Bedouin and there was live television coverage before, during and after the races. There was also a new breed of camel racing pundits who would opine on the likely outcomes.

Our Dubai rivals continued to pour massive sums of money into staying ahead, but the measure of our success would be how we performed at the annual racing festival held over three meetings in Dubai, Abu Dhabi and Qatar. They are spaced a month apart and run from January to March, while the weather is cool to mild. Each of the meetings runs over ten days. There are Gold Cups to be won for each age group and the biggest race of all is the Golden Sword, which is always the last race of the meeting. It is the ultimate prize, won by the best of the best of all the sheikhs' camels.

For the vets and the support teams this is a time of real pressure. With up to forty races a day and 270 races over a ten day period, it is possible for a trainer to have as many as a hundred camels running over a meeting. Then there is a two-week break between meetings before you have to do it all again. It's the time you prepare for your camels to be in peak form and free of injury.

Our performances had improved every year, picking up our first Gold Cup in 1996 and building steadily each year after that.

It was now 2000, twelve years after we had begun, and here we were on Dubai's home turf. The races were to be held at the Nad Al Sheba track, close to the centre of the city.

The sight was spectacular, a picture of modern Arabia all in one frame, with the centuries-old beasts of the desert set against the skyscrapers and glitter of a burgeoning Dubai.

It told the thousand-year-old story of Arabian transportation, from camels to Maseratis.

The 2000 Dubai racing festival became a milestone event for our science and training. No less than three of our camels ran as winners, one female and two males. All were products of the embryo transfer program.

Winning at home was important, but winning away, especially at the home of our rivals, was honey-sweet. If I had to name the breakthrough moment, the point where we moved from near-equals to leaders, this was it.

All that remained now was to win the Golden Sword.

Fourteen
Schemes and dreams

While Dr Alex Tinson, the camel vet, was succeeding in the job he had been hired to do, all along there was another Alex Tinson, who was living a parallel life of schemes and dreams and huge risks. This was happening under the banner of Harry the Camel, the children's book character I'd invented after the death of our baby, Natalia.

My dumb move to steal our camels from the former head of Interpol was symptomatic of the rollercoaster I was on, once away from the careful science of my day job breeding faster camels.

Harry the Camel had started as therapy. But this easy going, generous fellow, who liked nothing more than to snooze in the desert, became something else, something out of control. It was a case of one thing leading to another, leading to another. And then all of it—or most of it, anyway—crashing and burning.

Harry hit an early snag. He was originally called Harry the Lazy Camel, but this ran foul of the UAE authorities on the grounds that a camel was one of Allah's creations and so could not have any defects. So Harry the Lazy Camel became simply Harry the Camel.

The children's books in Harry's name definitely reflected what was going on in my desert vet life. They had started with a simple drawing of a camel and then spread to include all the wildlife I had come into contact with. The fearsome camel spider, Boris, became the bad guy in the Harry books. In the case of the graceful, mystical oryx, which had become a personal favourite of mine, I laboured hard to produce the most beautiful drawing I could.

I expanded on the first two Harry the Camel books with two more. The third told the story of Harry getting lost; straying from his desert home, he wound up in the mountains, where he met new species of beasts, such as the Arabian leopard. Harry ended up declaring that he never wanted to be lost again. I dedicated this book to Katya and Erica, my oldest girls. The fourth book depicted Harry's adventures on a trip to China and was dedicated to my dad.

From children's books I also started filing a regular weekly cartoon strip for Dubai's English-language newspaper; it too was based on Harry the Camel. The cartoons showed a more complex side to Harry and they often reflected how I was feeling, both good and bad. The cartoon strip, in turn, gave a great boost to the Harry the Camel books. Read by the UAE's expat population, this helped Harry take off as a multimedia personality.

I joined up with partners and next thing we were designing new versions of the Harry T-shirts. Then I expanded the T-shirt range to include other desert animals and we started selling the T-shirts at Dubai Duty Free, which gets a massive number of tourists.

My Harry-inspired enterprises were spreading far and wide. Tourists from all corners of the globe came to Al Ain for the camel safaris into the desert. Australian and American soldiers on R and R came along for the ride as well.

There was a touch of international glamour when *Vogue* magazine contacted us from New York to arrange a photographic shoot in the desert with model Heike Grebenstein in various poses with our camels. The shoot was made memorable when a Pakistani camel handler grabbed hold of Heike's bottom with one hand as he trailed behind her, camels in tow in the other hand. As she walked past us, Heike turned to me and asked, rhetorically perhaps, in her New York drawl, 'Is this guy meant to be holding my ass?'

Harry was on his way to becoming a superstar, and I was ready to ride the train. I lived with the feeling that life was short: I had direct experience that anything could happen at any time. It made me restless, needing to do more and different things.

I met with new partners who talked big about having the Walt Disney Company sign up Harry and take him to the world. We had exploratory meetings. We had follow-up meetings. We had planning meetings. We joined up with an international entertainment company as co-developers of the concept. We flew to the Philippines and commissioned animation projects. We produced a five-minute pilot of a Harry the Camel episode, which turned my one dimensional hand-drawn Harry into a walking, talking, potential television star.

In the fever of the moment we imagined we were onto something bigger than Bart Simpson. Ultimately, though, someone deemed that an American audience was unlikely to take well to a series set in the Middle East with the symbol of Arabia as its star.

I ended up losing a bundle on the Harry animation project that went nowhere, and it wasn't the only one. The thing about the UAE is that there's always an opportunist around who'll feed your dreams and take you for a ride. It attracts the hucksters and spivs of the world, like bees to a honeypot. Ultimately I was ripped off to the tune of hundreds of thousands of dollars because of my schemes and dreams. And it was always by other expats, never a local.

Losing money was one thing. Losing the plot was another.

If I had to pinpoint one moment when my Harry obsession might have got the better of me it was when I invented a camel language. It really was quite elaborate. I published a Harry the Camel diary, which offered 365 camel language words, one for every day of the year. They were all based around the 'cam' of 'camel'. 'Comments' became 'camments'. 'Cambay' was an Indian city famous for its film industry. 'Camtipasto' was a plate of mixed camel appetisers. 'Congratulations' became 'camgratulations'. 'Camilla Parker Bowles' needed no change to her name but was explained as a 'camtroversial' figure involved with a member of the British royal family. And so on, and so on. You get the drift.

To be fair to a man who was obviously in the grip of an obsession, this was my way of doing everything I could to take my love of camels to the world. The camel is always the animal shoved in the corner at the zoo. Knowing what I know about the camel, it stuck in my craw that it was taken for granted or, worse, seen as a bit of an oddity.

I knew there was so much more to them. I love the temperament of the camel, never skittish or panicky. You can see it in the way they keep their line when they cross a road: they don't care if a car comes along, they keep walking and don't get fazed and suddenly gallop off. If a camel gets caught in a barbed wire fence, it doesn't freak out but just waits for you to come and release it. A horse would thrash around, but a camel goes, 'You know what? I'll just sit here and wait.' They have the confidence to know they can deal with everything and an intrinsic intelligence that they don't get credit for.

Indeed, my infatuation with the camel was complete. And that's saying a lot for someone who is not given to emotional flights of fancy when it comes to animals.

My collecting of camel paraphernalia—or perhaps that should be 'camaphernalia'—took off. Pride of place above my bed was an original painting of our first embryo mother,

Sumha, captured in full regal pose in the desert. There were photos of our baby camels dotted through the house and frames of winning camels on the walls and cabinets. I found an old walking stick with a carved ivory handle shaped like a camel head, something that might have come out of *Raiders of the Lost Ark*. From Jordan I brought back a camel scene depicted in a glass case using layers of different coloured sands.

As I travelled the world on camel business I would invariably find more that took my fancy. There was a full camel saddle from Rajasthan. Also from India I brought back a long wooden bench seat with camel heads at either end. In Mongolia I was captivated by a two-humped camel carved out of a piece of tree root. From Turkey and Iran came floor rugs with various camel shapes embroidered in them.

On a trip to Paris I discovered a superb post-modern rendering in metal, which captured the essence of a camel in full gallop—I assume it is post-modern because most of the camel is missing, merely a hollowed-out body with the outer shell of a head, chest, front legs and hump, with tail flying behind. A case of less definitely being more.

Then there are the things from the Arabian Peninsula that go with a camel: the camel stick used traditionally to thwack a camel into line and the heavy silver chain used to pull a camel along.

If you did an inventory of my house you would find maybe a hundred different camel paintings, photographs, carvings, sculptures, embroideries and assorted accoutrements. At the whacky end, I acquired cloth camel heads to cover my golf clubs. If anyone's a camel tragic, it's me.

It may well be the case that my attempts to spread the word on my passion have fallen victim to some dodgy business dealings along the way. Fundamentally, though, I was well intentioned, a bit like Harry the Camel himself. I had to remind myself that the further I got away from my real scientific work with the camels, the worse I did. If I was faithful to that, it always repaid me, with success. Finally my frenetic, rampaging camel-mania crystallised into something that really did make sense.

I was at the point where I had proven my bona fides to the Crown Prince and his advisers beyond any shadow of a doubt. We'd had huge success with the breeding program and bit by bit we were delivering on the promise of producing champions that would win at major races, gradually chipping away at the dominance of our Dubai rivals. We had developed world-leading technology and techniques, which we were practising from superb facilities, carefully built up over years.

Flash Harry needed to be reined in, or at least have his energies directed elsewhere. It was time for my alter ego to go straight and for Harry to graduate from marketing and merchandising to something meaningful.

Harry was given a mission: to take a message of conservation to the world and make it a better place. It was time for Harry to go global.

Fifteen
Animal of the future

For most people, a camel is a goofy collection of body parts: knobbly knees; a droopy, drooling mouth; a ridiculously long neck that cranes and bends as though it has a life of its own. And a hump, of all things—not to store water, but as a fat reserve to survive without food in the desert. An improbable animal indeed, but then again you could say it is the only possible animal given the circumstances. I am happy to concede that the camel is one of the more unusual-looking of God's creatures. As a vet, though, the more I learned about the camel, the more complex the animal became and the more I wanted to know. I came to develop an endless respect for it. This is not to be confused with love—as I vet, I don't do that—but profound respect.

If you were going to design an animal from zero to survive in extreme conditions, you would come up with the camel. That's certainly the verdict of fifty million years of evolution.

Camels get a bit of flak in places like the north of Australia where they're seen as a pest. But its grazing habits make it perfectly in tune with its natural environment. It is a browsing animal; it picks here and there for its food and doesn't eat out an area. It moves around and comes back in circles. So, left to its own devices, it conserves its own environment. The camel doesn't damage its waterholes like cattle and sheep do. And in terms of its gut and ruminations it produces less methane, so it is lower on greenhouse emissions.

At a purely technical level, from top to bottom there is so much that is extraordinary about a camel. Its feet are padded and splayed so it can walk across the soft sand of the desert, rather than sink into it. It has three eyelids, rather than two, with the third acting as a backup wiper to remove sand and dirt.

The camel has an incredible series of adaptations that allow it to be super-efficient with whatever water it has. It has three different compartments in its stomach and moves water from one to the other as it's needed. It expels as little fluid as possible, excreting hard pellets of faeces after re-absorbing water in the large bowel and recirculating it. It has incredibly efficient kidneys that concentrate the urine to stop water loss.

The camel also has a mechanism to conserve fluid in extreme heat: its core temperature can go from thirty-seven up to around forty-one degrees before it needs to sweat, so it allows itself to get hotter than other animals. If it's sitting around in the middle of summer minding its own business, the camel will seek shade and orientate its body to minimise the heat it absorbs, then it will dissipate heat during the night, in time for the next hot day. The fact that it is built for sitting rather than standing means it has a lower heat profile.

Camels have a unique counter-current system at the back of their nose and near their brain, like an air-conditioner that exchanges heat so the blood travelling to the brain is the right temperature.

When a camel is dehydrated, you can witness them drinking a hundred litres of water at a sitting and watch them reinflate. No other animal can take in water at volume so quickly.

We humans would probably die if we tried this, because the sudden osmotic switch in our red blood cells would be so severe that they would rupture. The camel, unlike us, has spheroidal red blood cells, which can swell to 150 per cent of their normal size.

For me, the camel is the poster pin-up animal for conservation. It is the animal of the future, the animal of the twenty-first century.

Global warming means the planet is drying out. The deserts are getting bigger and water is a huge issue. For most people in the developed world desertification isn't really a problem, but for those who live in the forty per cent of the world classified as arid or dry, it is critical. The awful fact about the creeping spread of deserts is that it threatens the world's poorest populations in areas such as India and sub-Saharan Africa, making it even harder to reduce poverty. It is one of the greatest environmental challenges we face and affects about a third of the people in the world.

So one thing is for sure: the more the world turns into desert, the greater the need for camels. But at the same time, there are many parts of the developing world where the camel is endangered.

The UAE itself has had huge experience with saving desert animals that have become endangered because of increasing development or over-hunting. The oryx is a very good example. The Bedouin traditionally believed the oryx possessed mystical powers and that by eating them you would take on those powers. Consequently it was hunted almost to extinction. At one stage the oryx ceased to exist in the wild: by the mid-1980s there were only about a thousand oryx remaining, all of them in captivity, either in zoos or in private collections. The International Union for Conservation of Nature classified it as one of the most endangered animals in the world.

Private zoos like Sheikh Sultan's played an important role in saving the oryx from extinction. In one way, yes, his zoo was a showcase; but in another way it was the oryx breeding programs of Sheikh Sultan and others that helped build up their numbers. Between them the sheikhs have made good use of their private collections to this end.

While the camel embryo project was under way, we suggested we use the same technology to help restore the oryx population. For a while this was a serious proposition. Angus McKinnon and I flew over to London Zoo, the world's oldest scientific zoo, to learn more about capture and breeding techniques. We explored the idea of using the gemsbok, which is a species of oryx found in the Kalahari Desert, as the surrogate breeders. In the end the sheikhs decided this might be a distraction from the work of the camel program, but we were at least able to advise on ways to optimise oryx breeding.

As a result of all these efforts, the oryx became the first animal to revert to 'vulnerable' status after previously being listed as extinct in the wild. Populations have regenerated to over a thousand individual animals in the wild, and about seven thousand in captivity.

The President of the United Arab Emirates, Sheikh Zayed, was a conservation fanatic. From the late 1970s he built a latter-day Noah's Ark on Sir Bani Yas, an island off the coast of western Abu Dhabi. It was designed as a haven for Arabia's wildlife species that were endangered because of hunting or the pace of development. Dozens of species have been introduced to the island, including the gazelle, oryx, llama, rhea and ostrich. Many of these animals were classified as critically endangered or vulnerable. Sheikh Zayed also planted millions of trees on Sir Bani Yas, in an attempt to create a less arid microclimate.

So a dedication to conserving animal species very much existed in my own backyard. And one benefit of all my wild schemes was that, for all the money I had lost, I had nonetheless generated enough cash to fund some serious scientific work outside of the camel centre.

I felt that, while it was fine to use embryo transfer to produce superior racing camels, it would be wonderful if some of that technology could be applied in places like Mongolia or India, where there are endangered camel populations. The science that allowed us to accelerate the natural birth cycle of the camel had enormous ramifications for countries where the camel was facing extinction.

Poor populations need camels in all sorts of ways. They are a means of transport. They supply hides and milk. They can be eaten. Their dung can be used as fuel.

It wasn't part of my job to spread knowledge, but I thought that if I could do the research, come up with some practical spin-offs and write papers, then local government authorities or NGOs might take advantage of my work without having to put in the time and money themselves. I also had the idea that, while visiting these developing countries I could go to schools and introduce them to Harry the Camel and talk to the young about writing and environmental impacts.

Thus the HEF Foundation was born, to help 'Harry's Endangered Friends'.

My old mates from the early days of the camel centre, Heath Harris and Angus McKinnon, were fellow directors. The aim was to save camels around the world while also educating people about how to protect their camel populations and grow their herds. As a bonus, HEF would also allow me to pursue my passion for adventure, to get out of the lab and into remote places in exotic countries.

■   ■   ■

Embryo transfer had helped revolutionise Abu Dhabi's perform-ance on the track, but if Harry the Camel was to go out and do great work in faraway places then there was much more to be done.

The issue was how to tailor a lot of our hifalutin embryo transfer techniques into more practical solutions that could be used outside this big, flash multimillion-dollar facility we had. How can such an operation transfer to the desert, where there is no electricity, no sterile lab, and in fact pretty well nothing? How do you strip down the technology to the point where it could be taken into the field so it worked for the camel vet sitting on his own, with not much of anything, in a desert of Rajasthan or in the backblocks of Mongolia?

I also wanted the technology to be versatile, so it would work with all species of camel. This was not out of the question because ultimately the various species are somehow related, from the one-hump dromedary and the two-hump Bactrian, to the South American llama.

We fluked onto a solution by playing around in the lab with embryos at different stages of growth. A researcher from the nearby United Arab Emirates University was studying the rat embryo at every point in its growth, from six to thirteen days. Looking over his shoulder through the electron microscope, I could see that a six-day-old rat embryo and a six-day-old camel embryo didn't look a lot different and were about the same size. I suggested we collect a heap of camel embryos at various stages too, just to see what we got.

Normally we don't bother with embryos that are ten and eleven days old, because with most species the bigger the embryo gets, the more fragile it becomes. But we transferred a batch of older, larger camel embryos into some surrogates and, lo and behold, they worked very well. We theorised that the bigger the embryo, the greater was its capacity to trigger the ovaries to tell the camel, yes, you are pregnant. This produces more hormone and off you go.

This was an important discovery because it meant we could see the embryo and work with it without the need for a high-powered microscope. So, instead of the tiny, micro-scopic embryos we'd been working with for years, we had now discovered that larger embryos were actually easier to work with and led to the same or better results.

To transfer these bigger embryos we improvised with plastic artificial insemination straws, about the same width as a Bic biro. It meant we could suck up the embryo, load it up and whack it into the surrogate. We now had a cheap, practical way to do an embryo transfer in the middle of nowhere.

Our first destination would be Mongolia.

Sixteen
The ancient explorers' club

Just as the HEF Foundation was coming into life, across the world another camel fanatic was onto something very similar. An Englishman called John Hare had created a foundation with one mission: to save the wild two-hump camel found in the Gobi Desert. Fate again was making connections for me.

I knew John Hare's name well; after all, the world of camel fanatics is a small one. John Hare is one of those great British adventurers—men of empire who stoically, even cheerfully, venture into the most remote corners of the globe. John's home address was Kent, England, but his world was essentially wherever a camel could take him. He is one of those indomitable characters that Britain especially produces.

John had a colonial African background, something common to many in the British explorer class. He has the distinction of being the last recruit, in 1957, into what was styled as Her Majesty's Overseas Civil Service in northern Nigeria. In other words, he explored the African frontiers for Queen and country.

Much like my own experience with the Great Australian Camel Race, John developed an 'unreserved admiration' for camels when he first used them to cross the kind of terrain which is simply too tough for humans and their machines. John's many writings cover his extraordinary journeys by camel into the world's toughest environments. His first expedition was through little explored areas south of Lake Chad on the Nigerian–Cameroon border. A snippet from his writings gives you a flavour:

Unlike African porters, who had head-carried my kit from one place to another, my camels didn't complain about the distance or their pay. They didn't get roaring drunk on pay days, seduce the chief's daughter or need their feet dusting every day with DDT to prevent jiggers from laying eggs under their toe-nails. The porters were often very good companions but a camel could keep me warm on a freezing desert night if I had smeared enough kerosene over my body to keep its greedy parasitical ticks away. I ended those days of West African bush travel with great respect for the cheerfulness and stoic qualities of the porter, but with an unreserved admiration for the camel.

John Hare's singular passion was the wild two-humped camel, known as the Bactrian, which had become the eighth most endangered large mammal on the planet by the mid-1990s. It inhabited the Gobi Desert of north-west China and Mongolia, with a population numbering little more than a thousand.

A couple of years previously, John had received permission to enter China's former nuclear test site in the Gobi, where the wild Bactrian camel survives. No foreigner had been allowed to enter this vast, isolated desert area for forty-five years. Extraordinarily, the wild camel had survived forty-three atmospheric nuclear tests. It had also managed to survive on the salty, brackish water of the desert.

This is why I always say that if there's ever a nuclear holocaust or a meteor hits us, there are only three things that will survive: cockroaches, Keith Richards and camels. Everything else is rooted.

John had just established the Wild Camel Protection Foundation, with the renowned Jane Goodall as its patron. This was the British aristocracy of wildlife preservation. Jane Goodall had a neat phrase to sum up their unique joint venture: 'We are both basically creatures of the wild places and only leave them to save them.' Other patrons held titles from another age, such as the Marchioness of Bute, the Countess of Chichester and the Dowager Marchioness of Reading. They represented the old networks, which had the influence to tap into England's old moneyed class.

John and I first started talking via email. Though coming at it from very different directions, we shared both a passion and the aim of wanting to save endangered camel species. To both of us it seemed that the embryo transfer work I'd been doing might be if not the whole solution, then a good part of it. It was a proven technique for multiplying the breeding capacity. Given my interest in the endangered Bactrian camels of Mongolia, I thought this was perfect.

On meeting John in person I understood immediately what a massive concession to the modern age it had been for him to use this new-fangled thing called the internet to send an email. He came to stay with us in Al Ain. A tall, weather-beaten man, he lived up to the caricature of the great British explorer. He was already in his sixties but clearly had no plans to settle down in leafy Kent and see out his days in gentle retirement. Far from it. He was a fount of stories, and yet more adventures lay ahead of him.

John was in his late fifties when he made his early expeditions into the Mongolian Gobi and the Chinese Lop Desert and Gashun Gobi region, in search of the Bactrian camels. We often throw around the word 'epic', but in John's case it is the right description of the incredible trip he made. The Gobi is without doubt one of the world's harshest environments.

John and his team of locals endured more than a month out in that utterly unforgiving terrain, a barren, windblown moonscape where temperatures drop far below freezing point. He was the first foreigner ever to venture into these areas. He explained that, though in the company of a team, he actually preferred to travel by himself. And this man of another age had a rule that he would never carry a mobile phone on these journeys.

John's passion for the camel had come later in life but, having discovered it, he had more and more plans afoot to travel to ever more remote zones. He was already mulling over an expedition across the Sahara Desert, a venture which would take three and a half months to cover almost 2500 kilometres by camel. The route would follow an ancient camel route, notorious in the days of slavery as a road of extreme hardship and death. The last person to make the crossing was the Swiss explorer Hanns Vischer in 1906.

John was married, though with his many trips away he must have barely seen his wife and family. When he came to stay with us in Al Ain he brought along an old friend from Africa named Jasper Evans.

Jasper, too, was charming company and, if anything, even more of a camel nut than John. An Englishman who had lived most of his life in Kenya, Jasper had fixed a metal camel weathervane on top of his house in the Kenyan countryside, emblematic of the spirit that dwelt within. While John was the essence of English reserve, Jasper was a totally different proposition and more in the mould of the Kenyan cow-cockie. He was a short, energetic man who would turn up with a bottle of whisky for a long night of stories and jokes.

So here they were, foundation members of the ancient explorers' club, as I thought of them. John and Jasper were naturally keen to see the work we were doing at the Hilli research centre.

By this stage we had moved well beyond embryo transfer and had also produced the world's first frozen embryo camel calves. We were also close to two more world firsts: pre-sexed embryo calves and identical twin camel calves.

John and Jasper were staggered at the level of technology we were working with and the evident affluence of our surrounds. I think they might even have slightly resented the fact that all this highly advanced work was in aid of breeding faster racing camels.

But it was evident to John and Jasper that together we could work to regenerate the stocks of Mongolia's critically endangered Bactrian camel. And that's what we planned to do.

■ ■ ■

If you stay around the desert frontier town of Al Ain long enough, you are sure to meet extraordinary characters like John Hare and Jasper Evans. John and Jasper are examples of that very rare breed of westerner who turns their back on a conventional life and adopts the ways of the camel, holus-bolus. It is tempting to label them eccentric, but that's not fair. For them a camel is not just an animal. It is a way of life.

When you journey on a camel you unhook completely from all that is modern. Why would you bother with digital-age gadgets when you can take yourself off and immerse yourself in the most exotic parts of the world, areas which are inaccessible to human-made machines? You slow down. You see things missed from a car or a tourist bus whizzing by. It's just you, your thoughts and the rhythmic motion of the camel. Nothing else. In truth, most people can't handle that challenge. Above all, life atop a camel can give you a fabulous sense of independence from the props of modern life.

Of all the big characters I have met simply by being in the world of camels in Al Ain, the most remarkable is Michael Asher, another out of the great English adventurer mould. Michael has the distinction of having done more camel kilometres than anyone else in the world.

Michael came to Al Ain because he was writing a book about Wilfred Thesiger, the grandaddy of the British breed of desert explorers and Arabists. In the 1940s, in the company of the Bedouin, Thesiger made the incredibly arduous camel trek across the vast expanse of Arabian Gulf desert known as the Empty Quarter. This feat earned him the unending admiration of a young Sheikh Zayed, who later, as UAE president, honoured Thesiger with the adopted name 'Mubarak bin London', meaning 'the blessed one from London'.

But even though Sheikh Zayed, as tribal leader, had given Thesiger protection to travel through his lands, there was one tribe, the Al Dhuru, who had wanted to kill Thesiger as he made his crossing. Almost fifty years after Thesiger's crossing, Michael Asher wanted to know if I could help him make contact with the Al Dhuru tribe. He was planning to follow in Thesiger's footsteps across the Empty Quarter and wanted to rent half a dozen of my camels to make the trip.

Michael's infatuation with the camel began after he had served with the police anti-terrorist unit in Northern Ireland. Disillusioned with what he'd seen, he decided to make a big change. He moved to the Sudan in the late 1970s to work as a volunteer teacher and, while visiting a market, saw a camel for the first time. Straightaway he bought it and rode by himself for 1500 kilometres to join up with a camel train and make the journey to Cairo on the ancient caravan route known as the Forty Days Road.

Following that Michael lived for years at a time with Arabic-speaking tribes in the north of Africa and continued to make extreme camel treks. It gives you an idea of how much the camel was part of his life that five days after he was married he took his wife, the daughter of an Italian tank commander, to cross the Sahara Desert east to west by camel. He wrote a book about it called *Impossible Journey: Two against the Sahara*, which just about sums up what it must have been like.

Michael can trace a spiritual lineage that goes back to TE Lawrence, 'Lawrence of Arabia': British men who become captivated by Arabia and its world of survival and honour, centred around the camel. Indeed Michael Asher has written his own account of Lawrence's life as an Arabist.

Like Wilfred Thesiger, Michael shunned what the modern world has to offer. He didn't own a car—he didn't even know how to drive. He just wasn't interested. He came to believe that the industrialised world was necessarily a destructive force, sweeping away smaller civilisations, their cultures and their ways of living. It wasn't just an opinion or a position for the sake of a good argument. He lived and breathed his belief, formulated on top of a camel.

I was able to help Michael meet with the tribal leader he was seeking. We drove out to meet Owais, who lived a hundred or so kilometres from Al Ain in the deep desert. Owais was a very influential camel man, part of the older generation who had grown up hunting with a falcon from the top of a camel and defending his territory with a gun. He was a very tough, imposing character, but also quick with a laugh. Owais was perhaps in his late thirties when Wilfred Thesiger was crossing through Al Dhuru territory, and about seventy when Michael quizzed him in fluent Arabic on his recollections.

I had massive respect for Michael; he was a singular human being. Having said that, I doubt that many Emiratis themselves would go along with his or Thesiger's view that modernity is a bad thing for tribal societies. Thesiger predicted that the discovery of oil and the wealth that flowed from it would destroy the freedom of the Arabs to travel the deserts, to pick up their few possessions and go in any direction they desired. But if you speak to the Emiratis, I don't know if they would agree with that. I suspect they wouldn't. They'd say Thesiger was a dreamer and that he was projecting his romantic ideas on them.

The Emiratis have a way of looking at this through the lens of religion. They often say: we struggled for thousands of years and now Allah has rewarded us. Having lived for so long without the benefits of electricity or good medical care or air-conditioning, the Emiratis I know don't want to go back to the past.

I know too that I couldn't do what Michael has done, as much as I admire him for it. I rode a camel for a few days during the Great Australian Camel Race, just to get a sense of how tough it was for the competitors to make the three-month trek. I was left sore and limping, and glad to get off.

I knew my place and it wasn't on top of a camel for any extended time. It was far more likely to be behind, in front of, next to or leaning over it—wherever I needed to be to do my job as a vet.

And to be quite honest, I prefer to make my epic voyages in the comfort of a car or a plane.

Seventeen
Into the Gobi

No desert is easy, but the Gobi Desert of China and Mongolia is something else entirely. It is one of the least hospitable places on Earth. Now I was finally set to embark on my mission there: to put our improvised equipment to the test in harsh conditions outside the lab, and to secure access to a herd of endangered wild Bactrian camels, located on the border of Mongolia and China.

My new friend John Hare had documented his incredibly arduous journey across the Gobi in a book called *The Lost Camels of Tartary*, which I read to prepare for my trip. One small detail stuck in my mind: one of the great hazards was said to be the toilet pit, where the extreme cold freezes urine, forming an icy, pointed spike. So if you happened to lose your balance and topple over in the act, you risked being impaled. Or so the legend goes.

The great thing about following the camel trail, of course, is that it takes you deep inside a society. It gives you a chance to see firsthand the customs and ways of isolated populations.

I was looking forward to that as much as the challenge of bringing our breeding technology to a new frontier.

I had kept in touch with John and his ancient explorer mate, Jasper Evans, since they'd visited Al Ain, and also caught up with them at a camel conference in Beijing. There was the exciting prospect that we might travel together through Mongolia and start some programs to breed up the numbers of wild Bactrians.

Of course you can't simply waltz in to a foreign country and get started. You need permission from government and in a developing country like Mongolia there are a host of international NGOs working on agricultural, farming and wildlife programs. The idea was that John might co-ordinate our work through these organisations, but the bureaucracy and the paperwork proved to be difficult and time-consuming. I tend to be impatient to get things done so I decided to cut through the barriers and work directly with some well-placed government and university contacts I'd made. I might not have followed the rules, but it meant I could actually get something done.

There had been a huge international hullaballoo in recent years about the giant pandas being under threat. Yet at the same time the number of wild Bactrian camels had dwindled to the point where they were even rarer than pandas. This didn't quite capture the world's attention in the same way that cute bamboo-chomping pandas did, but the camel was in many respects more important, particularly to the local population, as a means of survival. Mongolians use the camel for transport, and to produce fuel, hair, milk and even meat in extreme circumstances.

Though the mission was to help save the camel, in this story it was the Bactrian that saved my life, literally. In fact, I nearly perished twice.

The capital city of Mongolia is Ulaanbaatar, and what a dreary, desolate and desperate place it was. 'Ulaanbaatar' means 'red hero' in Mongolian and that gives you a good idea of its heritage. Mongolia has a border with Russia on one side and China on the other. As the locals put it, they lived between the bear and the dragon; the challenge was not to get eaten alive by either of them. Mongolia was under the control of Soviet-era Russia for much of the twentieth century and this was reflected in the severe grey blocks of flats that had come to dominate the capital once the Soviet urban planners got to work in the 1950s.

Like other Soviet satellite states, Mongolia staged its own uprisings in 1989 and 1990. This led to democratic elections and a change to a market economy. Ulaanbaatar was a city still very much in transition year. Vast parts of it were so poor that families lived in the underground sewer network to escape the brutal freezing temperatures and the wind-whipped city streets. That's all changed now; today you'll even find Louis Vuitton stores there. But when I visited, it was nearly impossible to find a cappuccino, which is my ready reckoner for how remote a place is. After much searching I found one café that served a dismal, insipid cup.

Of all the places in the world to kick off with the HEF Foundation, this must surely have been the toughest.

The camel breeding season in Mongolia is winter, when temperatures have been recorded as low as minus sixty degrees Celsius. This would be the ultimate test for the new techniques I had developed to do embryo transfer in the wild, because at that temperature the embryo would instantly freeze.

So for this first trip the aim was more modest: I decided to conduct initial tests of how embryo transfer worked in the field not in the coldest winter months of December and January but in April, when conditions are not so harsh. One step at a time.

My main contact was a Mongolian man called Batsuri, who I had come to know through John Hare. Batsuri had a fine sense of humour and spoke good English, which was unusual in Mongolia. By day he was employed as a scientist at the Mongolian State University of Agriculture near

Ulaanbaatar, but he had a special passion to preserve the two-hump camel and luckily he had the means to pursue it. Batsuri's brother, who had apparently done well by owning shares in a vodka factory—what else?—agreed that embryo transfer could make a real difference and was prepared to put some money behind it.

Most importantly, with Batsuri as a partner in this venture I could cut through the red tape and get down to the real work of saving the camels. Batsuri had access to a herd of domesticated Bactrians we could experiment on before applying our techniques on the wild Bactrians. In the months before my arrival I had been in constant touch with Batsuri. I sent over vials of drugs and a very long list of instructions so that he could superovulate some of the females and also prepare a herd of surrogates to be ready to receive an embryo transfer. It was all timed so that I could check the results with this species of camel and carry out some embryo transfers in the field.

I spent a night or two in Batsuri's apartment in a grey Soviet high-rise before setting off to a farm a day's drive out of town, where our experimental Bactrian herd was kept. To describe it as a 'farm' is generous, if not downright misleading. It was, in fact, no more than an area of flat, stony desert completely devoid of vegetation, except for the odd small desert bush. The owner of this patch of dirt was a man called Poonsack, who was known locally as 'Rich Poonsack', for no other reason that in this desperately poor country he owned something, no matter how modest. As well as a large herd of camels, Poonsack ran a small number of sheep and dozens of goats.

Aged about sixty, Poonsack was in every way the traditional Mongolian farmer: physically tough from a life lived at the mercy of the elements, a real Genghis Khan character, and skilled in the ways of survival. When it came to slaughtering a sheep, he produced one of the most extraordinary manoeuvres I've witnessed. He rolled the animal onto its back, made a quick incision under the sternum, reached in through the abdominal cavity and grabbed the sheep's heart and held it. The sheep barely moved.

Poonsack had never visited the capital, Ulaanbaatar. He had had very little exposure at all to the modern world, yet it would turn out that he was quite partial to a night of karaoke, helped along with some vodka, of course.

Up close, the two-humped Bactrian camels were remarkable looking animals, much bigger than the racing camels I'd been working with. They had developed a thick woolly coat as an adaptation to the extreme cold. Altogether it gave them an enchanting air. Being a pack animal, they were more like the wild camels of the Australian outback. And of course it would not have been possible to open up the Silk Road trade routes that shaped much of Eurasia without the strength and endurance qualities of this breed.

We unloaded the box loads of ultrasound equipment, petri dishes, flushing fluid and flushing lines that I'd brought over from Al Ain and set up my new 'lab' in Poonsack's *ger*, a small, round Mongolian tent similar to a yurt. I balanced my trusty microscope on a wobbly old wooden table and set down a milk can behind it, which would be my lab stool for the duration. It was indeed a long way from the multimillion dollar research facilities of Hilli.

Batsuri's idea was that ultimately we would collect embryos from the endangered, wild Bactrian camels that were located a couple of days' travel away, and bring them in for transfer to the domesticated camels at the farm. Wolves posed a huge risk to Bactrian calves born in the wild so this place offered a safe environment. And it was a patch of Mongolia that we could control for our work, without the need for permits and permissions.

As a first step, it was essential to get to know the physiology of the Bactrian. Were there any differences to the Arabian or Australian camels I was familiar with? Even minor variations in the shape or size of reproductive organs would have an impact on how you could transfer embryos or flush them. So once again, I would spend a large part of my time at Poonsack's farm with my arm stuck up the rear of a camel, getting a feel, as it were, for what we had to work with. There were a lot of things to consider. Would we need insulation around the collection tube, for example, given that we would be moving embryos and fluid from the body heat of the camel to the minus degrees Celsius of the air temperature? The main aim, though, was to see if the superovulating drugs had worked and if there were any embryos fit for transfer. Back in Al Ain, this was a routine procedure. We had 'crushes' to immobilise the camel, with its rear towards me as I set to work from a stool. There was no such luxury at Poonsack's farm. We immobilised the camel by securing it with ropes while in its natural resting position: balanced on the knee pads of its front and back legs and its large sternal breast plate. A couple of the local boys held on tight, one at the rear and one at the head to stop it turning around. There was a constant threat of sandstorms so we positioned the whole operation behind an old stone wall, which would hopefully give us shelter. Then the tricky bit: with the camel in its resting position rather than standing up, there wasn't enough drop for the length of tube which syphons fluids from the uterus. The answer was to dig a metre-deep hole behind the camel, drop the end of the syphoning tube in there and have a helper lying on the ground with arms extended into the hole with tube in hand. Another helper stood behind the camel squeezing flushing fluids into its rear. Meanwhile, I was on my hands and knees, with one arm extended into the camel, on the top of its cervix.

As a gerry-built solution it was quite a sight, with locals hanging on to a nervous camel and two of us grovelling around on the dirt around a big hole in the ground, all against a backdrop of Mongolian *gers*, fences made of rocks and dozens of goats wandering around.

We had successfully improvised a way to collect embryos and transfer them. And that was quite an achievement.

Examining the embryos under the microscope, it was obvious that they were not as robust as they needed to be, so though we'd proven that you could superovulate a Bactrian there were still improvements to be made.

After close to a week at Poonsack's farm, I was satisfied that the basic technology worked, with some minor tweaks here and there. Now it was time for the second leg of the Mongolian mission: a two-day drive to the south-west of the country near the Chinese border, where I could see the wild Bactrian camel for the first time and talk with the local authorities about how we could breed up their numbers.

Batsuri and I returned to Ulaanbaatar and joined up with two professors from the University of Agriculture and three younger men brought on board to help with driving and the heavy lifting. We got two vehicles—one a serviceable Nissan, the other a slightly dilapidated Russian-built model—and set off.

Twenty kilometres out of the capital the bitumen ended abruptly; our link to even the most basic of civilisation was cut. For the rest of our trip we would not see another vehicle. Or even a single tree. It was flat, stony dirt all the way—like being on the moon.

I had absolutely no idea where we were going. There was no GPS. There were no signposts. You had to navigate by landmarks, such as a low hill in the distance. Sometimes there was no road at all, just the open plains of the desert. Any car that had been through left its own tracks, so there were tyre markings in every direction. We relied utterly on the knowledge of the local drivers, which was fine up to a point.

The weather in April should have been sensational. It was the very end of the winter season and, while you might still get the odd cold snap, it should have been nothing like the frigid conditions of December and January, when the country is largely snowbound, turning this region into a no-go area for outsiders.

At the end of day one of our journey there was a dramatic change. Off in the distance we could see a horrific black storm, and unfortunately it was heading towards us. We were in wide open spaces, with absolutely no protection and still some distance from any town. The Mongolians in the car were pretty cool customers, but I could feel a sense of unease building. You didn't need to understand what they were saying to know this was getting serious. Before long it became urgent.

We were still a couple of kilometres short of a place called Bulgan, a tiny little town in the middle of nowhere, when the storm started to hit. This wasn't rain: it was a black sand-storm, with tonnes of sand and stones carried by an enormous wind. When the locals get worried, you always know it's time for you to worry, too. All of a sudden, everything came flying almost horizontally at us. Sand and stone began to pelt against the windscreen as we made it into Bulgan. Quickly finding a hut where we could take shelter, we abandoned the cars and hustled inside.

There we spent two full days holed up with little else to do but play cards, drink vodka and hope like hell that our far from robust lodgings wouldn't get blown away.

As the black storm abated, we emerged to find that the town's one and only public toilet had been blown clean away. So now, in the tall tales and true of Mongolian adventures, I had my own toilet story to match John Hare's.

Some weeks later I came across an article in the *New York Times* that described this storm as the biggest and most devas-tating to have hit Mongolia in recorded history. The paper light-heartedly suggested that the force of the wind was so great that parts of Genghis Khan's DNA would now be landing in New York.

Having survived this near death experience, we cleaned off the cars, checked the engines for sand damage and continued on. What we'd experienced was dangerous, but worse was to come.

We were now four days into our journey, and heading towards the Altai Mountains in the Central Gobi; this is where the borders of Russia, China, Mongolia and Kazakhstan meet and is about as isolated as you can get. We were at the foothills of the mountains and beginning our ascent when, again, an uneasy feeling started to build in the car.

Our driver's local knowledge had managed to get us this far, but now it had run out and we were out of luck. He had lost his bearings in the open plains and wasn't sure if we were on the right road into the mountains. This might not have been a problem if it was the middle of the day and the weather was on our side. But that wasn't the case.

Before long we were again caught in a sandstorm. It was nowhere near as severe as the black sandstorm, but it was disorienting nevertheless. And now it was getting dark, and cold. Suddenly we were terribly exposed.

It was at this point that one of those moments occurred that makes you weep with relief. Two small boys riding Bactrian camels emerged as silhouettes out of the dust haze and sand. One of the boys was probably eight years old. His little brother was probably six. Our unlikely rescuers offered to guide us back to their father who, in exchange for some petrol for his motorbike, guided us to the main track up into the Altai.

We were on our way again, but now it was starting to snow. The temperature dropped, and it kept dropping the further we travelled up the mountain. We drove on and on into the gathering dark, with nowhere to stay and no idea where we were heading.

We knew the position was dire, but at that stage we didn't realise how close we were to complete disaster. Alarmingly, the temperature had now plummeted to minus thirty-five, and it was still only 6pm. We turned off the road and took a track leading who knew where.

By this time the snowstorm had become a whiteout. And then the gods smiled on us: we stumbled upon a small, round tent, much like Poonsack's *ger*. There was smoke streaming out the top: this was someone's home. And here was our shelter.

It turned out that no-one was home, but this was no time to stand on protocol. The seven of us piled into the empty hut and made it ours, a little like Goldilocks and the Three Bears comes to Mongolia.

The *ger* had a radio, some beds set against the walls, plenty of blankets, and a fire burning in a small furnace in the centre of the hut. We warmed up and gratefully settled in as the wind howled outside and the snow hit in ever-increasing waves.

At one in the morning there was a rustle at the door. The Mongolian family had returned from visiting nearby friends a couple of hundred metres away and a short dash through the storm. They were mildly surprised to find seven total strangers in their home but equally they were more than happy to share the space. In the desert, giving shelter to a stranger is a tradition—not just in Arabia, but the world over.

I always make sure I carry a small supply of goodies to give away when I'm on camel business in a foreign land, so I had some Harry the Camel T-shirts on hand, plus vodka, the local liquor of choice. A picture of a camel tends to create an instant bond with people who rely on them for their survival. Mongolians are also big on singing, so there we were in a tiny hut in the middle of the night, skolling vodka and launching into song as the wind and snow whipped around outside.

When we emerged the next morning it looked like we'd woken up at Mawson Station. There was a thick blanket of snow. And plonked down in the middle of it, calm as you please, were our host's Bactrian camels, quite unaffected after a night exposed to the most severe weather imaginable. We later learned that fifteen Mongolians had died in the area that night. We were very nearly amongst them because, if we had been trapped in the car, we would have frozen to death.

Our hosts gave us instructions on how to find a passable road for the final leg of our journey. Heading slightly north we negotiated a treacherous snow-covered track which led us to a rare bitumen road that had been cleared by the local authorities.

We had finally reached our destination: a designated preservation area for the wild Bactrian camel, at the top end of the Gobi Desert in a border area with China. We had planned to be there in good time for a special event: the birth of a wild Bactrian baby. But what with getting lost, being hammered by unseasonal storms and nearly perishing twice, our putative two-day trip had become a five-day nightmare. We missed the birth by two hours. Nevertheless, I was able to get a good look at both the mother and the calf, enough to see that they were quite different in appearance to the domesticated Bactrians at Poonsack's farm.

The local authorities had done their best to preserve the dozen or so wild camels that roamed across the reserve, which was actually an unfenced expanse of desert. They had managed to stop them straying into China or further afield in Mongolia by putting out food. But that was the extent of it. Otherwise the camels lived wild and were at the mercy of wolves and other predators.

Batsuri knew the local governor, who had arranged a series of meetings with the members of the local governing authority. He took the running on outlining our plans to breed up the numbers using embryo transfer with Poonsack's camels. There's no doubt the plan was feasible, but it was hard to get the message through that we could achieve the equivalent of twenty years of breeding in one year.

Meetings, meetings and more meetings. We left with an understanding that the local authorities would consider the proposition and that Batsuri would be the link man. This wasn't something that would be settled any time soon.

I left reflecting that I had gone to a lot of trouble for camels in my life, but I'd never before come this close to dying for the cause. If those two little kids hadn't turned up on their big woolly two-humped camels, we would have been history.

Eighteen
Guns and politics

When I redefined Harry the Camel's mission as a global ambassador for conservation, I hadn't reckoned on where exactly that might lead.

Populations that rely on camels are typically in the world's poorest areas, parts that can be lawless and dangerous. I'd had some experience of this while on a trip to Pakistan on official business for the Hilli Embryo Transfer Centre. We were in need of more camels to act as surrogates and Pakistan was a cheap source of supply and a place with close business links to the UAE. My trip on that occasion coincided with the 1997 election campaign, a fierce contest between the incumbent prime minister, Benazir Bhutto, and Nawaz Sharif.

Going to the bathroom in the home of a well-to-do Pakistani, I couldn't help but notice a Kalashnikov nestled between the basin and the bowl. And when my hosts left the house to go shopping they travelled with armed security, such was their fear of random attacks by Islamic extremists and/or political rivals.

It was 2001 and because of Harry's do-gooding, I found myself in another country and in yet another precarious position. This time I was huddled in the rear of a four-wheel drive on a single-lane road at 5500 metres travelling across the Khardung La pass, which winds through the Ladakh mountain range. Indian Army lorries were bearing down on us on their way to the Siachen Glacier, scene of the world's highest-altitude conflict, between India and Pakistan. Looking down a sheer 1500-metre drop, I could see the carcasses of trucks and buses that had fatally misjudged the room they had to make way for oncoming traffic. Everything about this latest camel mission was a white-knuckle ride.

The Khardung La pass was the only way to get to a herd of ninety Bactrian camels trapped in the Nubra Valley, one of the highest deserts in the world at over three thousand metres above sea level. The Nubra Valley is in the Indian state of Jammu and Kashmir, and bound by two of the world's highest mountain ranges. It's a picture-postcard spot, ringed by danger. Travel west a few hours and you'll be in Abbottabad, Pakistan, where US Special Forces found and killed Osama bin Laden. That gives you some sense of the tensions at play in this slice of the world.

The camels had been stuck in the valley since the 1960s, from the start of the Sino-Indian War. Prior to that, traders had used them as pack animals carrying goods along the Silk Road. But the trade had stopped because of the war and now the Bactrian's numbers had dwindled.

In the good times, the shaggy two-humpers trapped in the Nubra had been a major tourist attraction. But these were the worst of times. Tensions between India and Pakistan were high. Al Qaeda was threatening and the tourists had well and truly stopped coming.

Having road-tested the portable embryo transfer technology in Mongolia, I was confident our techniques would work in the field—even in very basic conditions at three thousand metres above sea level, so high that you need altitude sickness pills to work there. But the problem was that the herd was so small in the Nubra Valley there weren't enough female surrogates to work with and therefore build the population in any significant way. You might as well have simply mated the two-humpers with each other.

If there was to be a serious reproductive program, we needed access to another herd. The answer was down on the desert plains in the Indian state of Rajasthan where there were one-hump camels aplenty. These were biologically close enough that they could successfully carry the embryos of two-humpers. Indeed our Dubai competitors had successfully mated a two-hump and a one-hump camel and produced some fast camels, so we knew there would be no trouble in having one-humpers as surrogates to produce Bactrians.

Our plan of action confronted us with a second challenge: how to ensure that the embryos would survive a trip that might take two days, from the Nubra Valley to Rajasthan, in unpredictable conditions and without reliable refrigeration. We had done feasibility work on this in Al Ain, where we had experimented by leaving embryos in a holding solution out on a bench for up to thirty-six hours at room temperature. We discovered to our delight that there was no impact on the transfer rate. So, with some fancy footwork we had improvised a scientific solution that worked. All we needed now was to get our hands on the Bactrian camels.

I had been working with Indian colleagues to negotiate with the local government department responsible for the Nubra Valley camels so we could procure half a dozen or so for the project. The camels were owned by various tribal leaders, but government officials would have the final say. My ultimate vision was to set up a specialised research centre here to regenerate the herd and to use camel rides to fund it. A new international airport was being built at the nearby town of Leh and it seemed to me that the tourists might one day return.

The only things that could stand in our way were bureaucracy and local politics, and this meant finding a way through a maze of agencies and petty officials. They proved to be impervious to the logic that we had the only embryo transfer technology in the world, that I had adapted it to work in the field and that this could help save the local herd for future generations.

In the end, the government hierarchy took the view that there should be an Indian solution for an Indian problem. This was one of the frustrations of working in places that might need assistance: the government gets in the way. As with Mongolia, I was determined to find a solution. The only way around this particular block was for me to train Indian vet students in the art of embryo transfer through lectures and demonstrations. And so, HEF India was established with a clutch of powerful local politicians on board. There would indeed be an Indian solution for an Indian problem.

Although this was not as straightforward as I had originally hoped, I still found we could do a power of good. I was able to sponsor the publication of a camel journal through the Haryanna Agricultural University, to engage Indian vets in the techniques of camel breeding and conservation. I was also able to stump up money from our HEF fund so books could be provided free to students; as well, we supplied ultrasounds, gloves and other equipment needed to carry out embryo transfer.

■ ■ ■

The danger of getting into Nubra was only matched by the danger in leaving it.

On the way to the airport at Srinigar, we stopped over at the Dal Lake for a short stay on a houseboat; of the seventy houseboats on the lake, we were the only customers. The guest book showed that Charlton Heston had once stayed here, an echo of another era before terrorism arrived.

At the once-glorious Oberoi Hotel, too, there were no other guests and we were waited upon by dozens of underemployed Kashmiris, watching their livelihoods go down the drain because of conflict and local terrorism.

In the city of Srinigar the Indian authorities enforced a 9pm curfew, and there were machine-gun nests and sandbags on every corner. 'Trouble in paradise' doesn't even begin to capture the air of menace. I felt like I had a target painted on my head. It was truly scary stuff.

When it came to leaving, I encountered airport security like I have never seen before or since. I was searched before entering the airport grounds, then all batteries had to be removed from devices before check-in. And, as we passengers walked across the tarmac to the plane, security checked us again. But they were, after all, trying to counter a terrorist group prepared to drive bombs through the periphery fence.

Five days after leaving Srinigar, the reason for the heightened security became clear. I was transiting through Hong Kong and running late to get to my gate, which was at the end of the terminal. As I belted along I looked up at a television screen and saw something horrific unfolding. A plane was flying into a skyscraper in New York. And then another plane crashed into a second building. For a moment I thought it was a movie, until I heard the commentary.

The date was the eleventh of September 2001. Life in the Middle East was about to change. And before too long, so was mine.

Nineteen
The Dad trail

My family life was fraying around the edges. Patti and I decided to call it quits but, thankfully for both of us, our three daughters remained our central concern.

Our decision to send our oldest girl, Katya, to boarding school in Melbourne had turned into an unmitigated disaster. She was having a terrible time.

The idea had been to put some distance between her and Khaled, as well as to give Katya the best possible education for her final two years. In reality, though, she suffered terrible anxiety being separated from Khaled. She was lonely; she was all at sea being away from her family. In short, Katya missed the place and the culture she called home. Indeed, things got so bad for her that she almost needed to be hospitalised.

This is one of the occupational hazards of being an expat. If you stay away long enough, it becomes harder and harder to know where home really is. In Katya's case it wasn't about a lack of anchors. She was just marooned in the wrong place.

Meanwhile, things weren't much better for Khaled. At the age of eighteen he was sent to university in San Diego, where there was a community of Emiratis who would hopefully watch over him. However, there was something else going on.

Katya and Khaled were, in fact, continuing to keep in touch regularly. On one occasion Khaled took a flight out to Australia from San Diego to see Katya, who was now in Melbourne and staying with Patti. The two of them had pretty well disregarded everything I had said back in Al Ain.

I'm not the sort of parent to pull out the big stick, but we were trying to handle a very delicate situation. After Khaled's dash to Melbourne it was made clear to them that enough was enough. Katya knuckled down to complete her high school exams while Khaled stayed in the States to complete his studies.

We were sure that this meant the end of the line for Katya and Khaled, but I hadn't counted on how determined they both were. Or perhaps I failed to comprehend how much each of them meant to the other. I was certain that their relationship could have no future so, as much as anything else, I feared for the pain both of them would feel if they continued to ignore their families' wishes. In retrospect, it really just shows that you can't interfere in your kids' lives too much because you can mess things up badly.

The welfare of my daughters played constantly on my mind. I was aware, too, of my persisting problems in coming to terms with the premature deaths of two of my daughters. Some people had trouble understanding why I was so concerned about the physical safety of my girls. I might worry about the sort of car one of them was driving, or the kind of part-time job another of them might want to take on. Did it put them in danger? The episode when Katya was nearly hospitalised in Melbourne rattled me, which was why I flew out to spend several weeks with her at that time.

I couldn't bear to lose another child. I think it would have broken me.

Of course, Patti and I were aware that we weren't the only

ones who'd lived through the deaths of our two little babies. Katya and Erica had known loss and grief from a very young age. Madeline had been spared the firsthand experience of losing a little sister but, of course, her life was also deeply affected by it. I was aware that it had left all our daughters with a similar sense of life's impermanence and an apprehension from a tender age that babies didn't necessarily survive. As a parent, there's no manual on how to handle these things. You just do your best to preserve a sense of family.

Yet that was splintering. Madeline was only twelve—and eight years younger than Erica—when Patti and I split up. Maddy stayed with her mother and our lives were becoming separate, much as I tried to keep up contact.

That's perhaps one reason why it was important to me to bring Erica along on the Dad trail: to travel to Shanghai to see where my father had lived as a child.

■ ■ ■

While we were living in the UAE, Dad had passed away in Australia at the relatively young age of sixty-five. So much of what I had done was to live up to my father's adventures. I wanted to honour his life.

I'd always had a dream that Dad would take me back with him to China. I imagined he might show me the alleyways where he'd played, the school he'd attended and so on. That never happened and really I wonder if he could ever have overcome his awful memories and made the journey back.

I wanted a sense of the place to match my imaginings of what life was like for Dad as a teenager in a Japanese POW camp. All I had to go on was Steven Spielberg's movie adaptation *Empire of the Sun*, which depicted the experiences Dad lived through, down to counting the weevils in the rice ration he was given in the camp.

Dad had given me so little detail of where he lived, but I managed to piece it together going on a description from a good mate of his who was in Shanghai at the same time. When Erica and I visited Shanghai, I believe we located it: a big, three-storey colonial home in the French concession. Extraordinarily, it was as though Dad's old neighbourhood was frozen in time. It was remarkably intact. Spielberg has said that when he made *Empire of the Sun* in the mid-1980s, he only had to cover up some advertising boards for everything to look the same as in the 1940s.

On one side of the Huangpu River, which flows through Shanghai, is the China of the twenty-first century with its glitzy high-rise towers. Directly facing it on the other side is the old Shanghai Bund, which includes the International Settlement, unchanged from when Dad lived there as a boy. It was like stepping back into the colonial era, when Britannia ruled the waves. Grandpa's office was still there in the building that housed the giant shipping company Swire, now trading as the China Navigation Company.

Erica and I sought out the hotel and clubs where Dad and his family used to hang out, living the expat life of parties and big family gatherings. Dad loved the piano and one of my favourite memories is of him playing Beethoven's 'Für Elise'. We went to a hotel where I knew Dad would have gone as a kid with his parents and asked the pianist to play it. A couple of times. Erica and I raised a glass to the father I loved and who had loved his family so much.

But the trip to Shanghai served other purposes besides tracing Dad's early life. I needed to check-in on progress with the Mongolian embryo transfer program and also to speak to students at the State University of Agriculture, so we tacked on a trip to dreary Ulaanbaatar for HEF Foundation business.

Of all my girls, Erica seemed the most likely to follow in the Tinson tradition and become a vet. As a little girl on the Gold

Coast she had happily tagged along on house calls with me. Growing up in Al Ain, she was both curious and fearless when it came to the snakes and lizards. She had even coped well when Boris, the fearsome camel spider, made an unscheduled appearance in her bedroom one night.

I wanted to give Erica the opportunity to experience some of the things that life as a vet had to offer. It could mean giving the best treatment to domestic pets, or it could open up new horizons and make a difference to people's lives. It all depends on the spirit you bring to it and the sort of person you are.

We met up with Batsuri and made the trip out to old Poonsack's farm. On the way we were caught in yet another unseasonal storm, though this time, thankfully, it was milder than on my first trip.

Batsuri had made impressive progress. He had built a two-storey timber structure on the farm, with a lab occupying the bottom floor and kitchen and sleeping quarters upstairs. He had fitted out the lab with bench tops and an area to walk the camels through to make the embryo transfer process efficient. He also had a designated area for a crush to keep the camels immobilised. All in all it was a big step up from my first visit when we'd dug a hole in the ground and had the camels restrained by locals as goats wandered by. I had also sent a bunch of microchips on to Batsuri so that he could organise with his contacts at the reserve in the south-west of the country for their dozen pure bred wild camels to be tagged. For Erica's benefit I was tempted to get Poonsack to perform the Mongolian sheep slaughter but thought better of it.

Batsuri rolled out the red carpet this time. At the university I was given an official welcome prior to speaking to the students on reproduction techniques. Batsuri had also organised for two pure white Bactrians to be presented to Erica and me. Sadly, though, we couldn't take them with us.

Other young women might have found this all too tedious. But it was evident to me that Erica had the spirit of the wild.

Twenty
Time to go

I loved the unpredictability of my life. Every day I had to be ready to throw away the script and take off to wherever I was needed, whether it was attending to a sick cheetah at a sheikh's private zoo or checking out a camel for sale in Saudi Arabia or Qatar. Unpredictability had generated a lot of benefits for me, but now, after fifteen years in the UAE, it was my turn to experience its downside. I had no warning of what was coming.

I was contacted by Sheikh Sultan and told that the Hilli centre would close. As far as our high-tech reproductive work was concerned, that was it. Staff would be redeployed elsewhere. Everything we had built up over more than a decade would be shut down, lock, stock and barrel.

There was no official reason. The scientific work was flourishing, we had established a reputation as the leaders in reproductive technology, and our camels were winning important races. It was hard to understand.

I was given the option to stay on and continue with routine work, like the treadmilling, and collecting and analysing blood for the trainers. I could keep being paid, but professionally my interest had always been in pushing the genetic and scientific boundaries.

There had been an ongoing sense that the success of the embryo transfer program had bred jealousies and some resentment from local trainers. It was possible that our camels had proven a threat to the old system, whereby Sheikh Khalifa would buy promising young camels from the Bedouin. Now he could get superfast camels bred in the lab. So maybe there was a perception that we were interfering with the informal wealth redistribution structure. None of it was clear to me, but I was pretty sure the centre was a victim of its own success. There had always been a chance that this might happen. That was all part of being in a country where you didn't quite belong.

Whatever the reason for the decision, at this point I wasn't thinking long-term. I decided to go but I didn't want to burn my bridges, so we agreed that I would always be available to come back if there were any special projects where I was needed.

However, before leaving the service of the sheikh, he did me a huge favour, which would come in handy in later years: he gifted me four excellent breeding camels. Here's how it came to pass—and I must admit, it did involve a little bit of chicanery on my behalf.

Sheikh Sultan decided that he would make a generous offer to the local Bedouin: he would give them four good camels for any four camels they brought in, whether they be good, bad or indifferent. This gesture to the Bedouin was an example of how the tribal system continues to be the social glue, despite the modernising of the Emirates. There is a social contract between the rulers and the ruled, and it is this contract that sustains the respect and support of the locals.

Naturally, word of the sheikh's trade-up offer spread far and wide. The very best camels from the sheikh's herd were being reserved for the sheikhs of other local tribes, but there were still many excellent racing camels on offer.

Of course, I had unparalleled inside knowledge, so I grabbed four young camels that I knew were well bred and good embryo transfer responders and stuck them in a corner, hoping I could somehow get in on this deal too, despite the fact that the sheikh's offer was intended only for the locals. Every time someone arrived with their dud camels they'd see the four flash camels in the corner and ask if they could take them. I'd tell them that they were already reserved for a VIP.

Finally the sheikh agreed that I could be part of the deal because I had been there for so many years. At that point I got hold of four run of the mill camels and exchanged them for the four really good ones I had put to one side. I was on the point of leaving Al Ain and I wasn't sure when—or if—I would be back, so I arranged to have them kept at a camel camp near town.

The camels were microchipped, which would be very important later on when it came to proving that they really were my camels. It's a good thing they were, because those camels ultimately turned out to be a smart acquisition.

■ ■ ■

I was reluctant to leave the UAE. It was home. The girls no longer lived there but it held strong memories as the place where we had raised them, and I had good friends amongst both the Emiratis and the expats. I had also come to enjoy the perks of the expat lifestyle that comes with success in the Gulf, like being able to jump on a plane to London or Paris for the weekend. And besides, there was HEF Foundation work to be done in nearby countries like India and Iran.

Maybe because I was losing my link to the camels, I found some familiar demons gathering again. The restlessness to do more and different things returned. I had an impulse to keep moving, to make the most of every minute in case life should suddenly come to a halt. Was it driven by the sudden death of our two babies? Was it simply that I was born impulsive? Or was it the cliché midlife crisis? You wonder if there is more to life than what you have, even if what you have is pretty good. Maybe I just wanted to keep challenging myself. I'm sure there's a psychology PhD in unravelling all that.

I decided to stay on for a period in Dubai, the UAE city where almost anything is possible. In my optimism I rekindled some old plans for Harry the Camel, but in the end nothing came to pass and my new adventures in the world of business went down the drain. Again I found myself being ripped off by people I believed I could trust.

The last venture to bite the dust was an antique business in Dubai in which I had a forty per cent stake. The business was a victim of trouble in the region, following on from the September 11 attacks. When President George W Bush led the 'coalition of the willing' into Iraq, the tourists stopped coming. They had a misguided sense that bombing Baghdad, thousands of kilometres away on the other side of the Middle East, might somehow mean carnage in the UAE. Go figure, but such is the panic that mere mention of the word 'Arab' can induce.

By now I had been living in the UAE for close to fifteen years. Compared to most expats, that was a marathon stint, but it was clear that time had run out for me. I salvaged what I could from the ruin of my latest business failure, loaded up a container full of antiques and headed for the exit.

I make quick decisions and they're not always the best ones. But I just needed to move. I was closing in on fifty years of age and I was a man without a plan.

Twenty-one
The returning son

Since leaving for Al Ain in 1988 I'd made regular trips back to Australia, but with each passing year I felt increasingly detached from where I was born and raised. At my core I remained Australian, but it felt less and less like home to me.

It's wonderfully liberating to live a life between two continents. In a way you feel special in both: in the land of your choosing you are a foreigner and in the land of your birth you can be the returning son, coming home temporarily from time to time with exotic tales of a faraway place.

Coming back to Australia now, though, my wings were well and truly clipped. There was no hopping on the next plane out. After years of earning good tax-free money, my latest business exploits in the UAE had left me pretty well broke. I didn't even have enough money to clear my container of antiques from the wharves and needed a loan from my family.

I set up home in Wangaratta, about seventy kilometres south-west of Albury on the Hume Highway. Mum had been living there since Dad died and it was within striking distance of the old family winery. After years of living in a frontier town, where fascinating strangers might wander in from the desert, frankly it felt dull.

I saw, too, that life was not easy for most people. There was this thing called a GST and another called income tax—all the nasty parts of life in Australia I'd forgotten about. More than I had remembered, life in Australia seemed so orderly and ordered that it sucked the life out of life. Over and above all of that, Australia felt oppressive, with rules and regulations stifling everything.

The common stereotype is that making one mistake in a country like the UAE could be fatal, but the opposite was the truth. The important thing was to be honest with the sheikhs and to make an honest effort. I couldn't imagine in Australia having the same opportunities I'd been given in Al Ain to experiment and perhaps fail with a big new venture.

I was a world expert when it came to camels and had co-authored a compendium on them for the University of Sydney's Post Graduate Foundation in Veterinary Science. This A to Z on the physiology of camels represented a decade's knowledge gained in the camel capital of the world and became a bible for students in Australia and internationally. Want the lowdown on ampullae? There it is on page twenty-six. Curious about zoonotic diseases? There are sixteen of them, listed from pages 297 to 299.

Back in Australia, though, this counted for little. My vet registration had lapsed, so I needed to apply again. There was no need for me to sit for an exam, but I hadn't done work with cats and dogs for fifteen years. If somebody had turned up with a sick camel, cheetah or a timber wolf, no problem. But I mightn't be much help if Mrs Smith's cat had a sneeze or a wheeze.

The practice of veterinary medicine had changed a great deal in fifteen years. There were new techniques and equipment, such as anaesthetic machines with monitors attached. So I had to bluff my way through my first few locums just to get on top of things. There was a new attitude, too. People were prepared to pay hefty sums, up to six or seven thousand dollars, for treating their pet. Fifteen years before, five hundred dollars was considered too much.

I wasn't being paid a huge amount as a locum and the work wasn't regular—if no vets were taking any holidays then there was no work for me. I love unpredictability but this was the uncomfortable kind: where to find the next dollar. So I took locums wherever they came up, in vet clinics all over Australia—from Melbourne, across to Alice Springs and Perth. I was effectively living out of the back of a four-wheel drive, moving from one temporary job to the next. It was a good way to see Australia again, and I enjoyed the work when it came along, but in truth it was not what I was best at, and that made me feel vulnerable. Dogs and cats might not be my thing, but they deserve the best care they can get.

My youngest, Madeline, was now living in Florida with Patti, who had remarried. On the bright side, though, I could be near Katya, who was working in Melbourne, and Erica, who was now studying at Melbourne University. She had finally come to the conclusion that she wanted to be a vet. As an alternative, she had contemplated a science degree, which sounded like a good idea to me; as a scientific researcher with a multinational company there would be the opportunity to make serious money. I cautioned Erica that as a graduate vet she'd get paid less than fifty thousand dollars a year in an intern job to begin with, and then not a whole lot more later, unless she was able to do the hard yards and set up a profitable practice, a process that can take a long time.

Erica went ahead anyway. Maybe it had been that trip to Mongolia. Maybe it was growing up surrounded by exotic and weird creatures with a mad vet as a father. Maybe it was just the power of the Tinson genes.

I was quietly pleased with her decision. All our girls loved animals, but Erica was probably the most like me in her temperament and the way she approached an animal. The Tinson family tradition would continue.

■   ■   ■

At the time, my decision to leave the UAE had seemed completely logical. But now I wondered what had possessed me to throw in working for one of the world's wealthiest men with all the privileges that came with it.

I was really struggling, in every way.

I'd go to gatherings with old mates from school or uni days and try to keep a stiff upper lip. But all the while I couldn't escape the terrible knowledge that I was in the deepest financial trouble of anyone in the room. These were the times when I would question all the major decisions I had taken in my life and my compulsion to keep moving in search of bigger and better adventures, to follow my wild dreams. If I hadn't said 'yes' to Heath Harris's offer all those years ago, might I now have been better off? I had come to live by the maxim that he who dies with the most good stories wins and, sure, I had accumulated a great trove of experiences, but what use were they to me now?

My mates had run a steady race. They'd stayed in one place; they'd been married for twenty-five years; they had their houses in St Ives, worth a small fortune; and by and large they had happy families, with kids from stable homes ready to set off to university and start the cycle all over again. And what had I done? I'd been to Mongolia, to Ladakh and to Rajasthan. And now here I was with a big fat nothing. It was a terrible feeling, and I did everything I could to hide it from my mates.

Mostly my friends didn't realise how bad things had become, or they didn't want to ask. But one of my dearest friends, Frank, sensed something was wrong and called to ask if I was all right. I replied that, yes, everything was fine, no worries. However, a couple of days later I rang him back. I swallowed my pride and asked him if he could lend me a couple of thousand dollars, to get me through a particularly tough patch. Later, when the wheel turned, I was able to give Frank a beautiful Kashan carpet from Iran, which I am glad to say more than repaid my debt to him.

For a year or so I lived a hand-to-mouth existence. It was pretty ordinary. I remember very clearly when the lowest point came.

I had nothing in the bank. I had no credit left, except on one card which was always maxed out. For the first time I understood the full meaning of the credit card trap and got a sense of why so many others only just managed to survive. Walking past a café in the main street in Wangaratta, I put my hand in my pocket and realised that all I had was $1.75. I couldn't even afford a coffee. I was at zero—and I feared it was going to get worse.

But, no matter how broke I was, I refused to sell my antiques. Camels and antiques were my great obsessions and they were intrinsically linked, given the camel's role in trade across the Middle East. I had slowly gathered a great collection: swords, guns, cabinets, Syrian furniture, Portuguese pieces out of Oman, chests, boxes, carved doors, carpets and silver goods. I always feel that the objects we gather around ourselves reflect who we are, more so than our houses. Most of these things represent key points in our lives, both the highs and the lows. When I'm happy, I spend money. And when I'm pissed off, I spend money. I appreciate the concept of collecting and I like the idea of buying quality stuff, which can be passed down from generation to generation. This was more important to me than cashing them in to get by.

I realised the only chance I had of coming back from the brink was to return to Al Ain. But I also knew I couldn't make the first call.

Thankfully, the wheels of destiny were about to turn again.

When you want something badly enough and you finally get it, you will always remember the exact moment when it arrives. I was getting out of my car outside my brother's vet clinic when my mobile rang. It was my old manager at the Hilli research centre calling. It seemed that since I left there had been zero high-tech breeding or research—everything had come to a halt. He called to relay the news from Sheikh Sultan that the embryo program needed to start up again.

Not for the first time, the camels had come calling. The difference this time was that I knew one hundred per cent what that meant. And I was hanging out for it.

Not that I let on.

Twenty-two
City boy to desert nomad

When I returned to Al Ain I realised immediately how much it had become part of me, and me of it. You might say it was my destiny.

I even managed to find the sign that my old friend Yafour had knocked up for me almost fifteen years before as I had put the finishing touches on the Tinson family home. There it was, discarded in some building rubbish out the back: 'WARNING! Reduce speed. Children and camels around.' The family was no longer in the house, but here was a sign, surely, that I was back where I belonged. I dusted off Yafour's handiwork to reveal the familiar white lettering on red-for-urgent background and leant it up against a wall at the entrance to the driveway.

In my absence the house had been occupied by Sheikh Sultan's son, who had decked it out in hues of red, black and gold and shipped in huge luminescent blue lounges and ornate ivory-coloured bedheads. Some might call this garish; I loved it all. But the young sheikh had removed the various aquariums I once used to house my collection of snakes and lizards. I would have to reinstate a new collection, just to feel completely at home.

Returning to Australia had been a transformative moment: I discovered that I didn't belong there anymore. I felt safe back in Al Ain and not just in a financial sense, as important as that was. It defies the stereotype so many outsiders hold of the Arab world, but I actually felt physically safer. When people see conflict in the Middle East, they assume you could be killed any minute by a gun-toting, wild-eyed extremist. But that couldn't be further from the truth, especially in the UAE where internal security is uncompromising. With my network of old Emirati friends I also felt I had a safety net of protection if anything should go wrong, financially or in any other way.

And maybe, above all, I felt safe because I was doing what I was designed to do.

I took myself off to catch up with the trainers out at the various camel camps and renew my acquaintance with them. Over the years the camps had been my office, the place where I plied my trade. I guess I had regarded them in very practical terms—as functional places for animals. I had become familiar with them to the point of being blasé about how truly exotic they were. But now coming back to them, just for a moment I was able to see them with the eyes of a newcomer.

In one corner of the enclosure camels sat as a group on the sand, their legs tucked neatly under their bodies, all dressed in their patterned blue cotton covers, secured with rope under their bellies. On their muzzles were red, coarse-knitted covers resembling a tea-cosy to stop them from ingesting stones or sand should they attempt to graze between feeding times.

If anyone approached, one would let out a long, low, guttural grunt, a sign to the rest that a stranger was around. Others in the herd would slowly crane their necks to take in the intruder before returning to their business. In another part of the enclosure the camel boys stood by their charges, holding onto them with rope tethers as the camels bent their necks low to scoop up feed.

Across the way groups of camels in their threes and fours stuck close together, were mooching slowly across the red sands behind the lead camel, with a camel handler sitting cross-legged atop. As the sun descended, the handlers and their camels turned into silhouettes, shrinking smaller and smaller until they flickered out of sight.

Heath Harris had always said the UAE was like a giant film set, and so it was. No other setting can conjure images like this. I understood then that I was a city boy who'd become a desert nomad.

Being the one westerner amongst the Bedouin was something I had always cherished. It was like this out in the desert, where we might have set up a camel camp or just be sitting together around a fire. I could have a decent conversation about most things in Bedouin Arabic, which made me feel that I had a rare connection. At the same time, it made me aware that I was different.

If I think about it, I've always gravitated to being alone in the middle of nature, whether it be in the bush, the desert or even the ocean. But the desert has a special sort of emptiness. In the golden sand and brilliant blue sky there's a feeling of tranquillity and a sense of quiet power. The silence is complete and enveloping. The landscape is stark, and beautifully so. In its vastness you feel small. Its tranquillity overwhelms the agitation of your thoughts. The desert is a time as much as it is a place.

The camel looks regal in these surroundings. It belongs there. And so do I.

■　■　■

There had been a convulsive change during my absence. The President of the United Arab Emirates, Sheikh Zayed, had passed away. For thirty-three years he had ruled the UAE and guided its development through extreme change; the majority of Emiratis had known no other leader. They had a relationship with him that is unknowable in a western democracy, where prime ministers and presidents come and go.

One major consequence was that my ultimate boss, the Crown Prince, Sheikh Khalifa bin Zayed Al Nahyan, had been elevated to the office of president. I would therefore be responsible to the most powerful man in the country. Ultimately this would have implications for the scientific research.

The change posed big questions. What direction would the country take now? Would a younger generation of leaders care less for the old ways? In short, the UAE was at a crossroads.

Sheikh Zayed's death had brought a time of reckoning for the country. Sheikh Zayed was the symbol of old Arabia, and seen perhaps as its custodian. It is almost impossible for an outsider to understand the reverence and affection that the Emiratis had and continue to have for Sheikh Zayed.

I was given a glimpse of this at the first races I attended in the days after I arrived all those years ago, when dozens of men had surrounded the sheikh to show their respect and adoration. It was a scene I saw repeated many times over. When his death was announced on Abu Dhabi television, the newsreader broke down in tears and was unable to complete the report.

When Sheikh Zayed was born in 1918, there was no such thing as the United Arab Emirates, just a collection of tribes clustered around various powerful families who controlled swathes of the desert. For much of his life the locals were dirt poor, living in huts made of palm fronds and washing themselves by rubbing sand across their bodies. They survived extreme heat and severe winds without relief. Those on the coast made a living out of diving for pearls, but this was dangerous work and for little reward. It was a time of no electricity and therefore no air-conditioning against the fifty-degree-plus heat, so in the summer families living on the coast would make the trip inland to Al Ain across the desert by camel, to escape the unbearable humidity. It was a journey of more than a week and it was not uncommon for some of the old and the very young to die on the way.

In the time before oil transformed the UAE, Sheikh Zayed would travel by camel around the Abu Dhabi emirate. The discovery of oil, of course, changed everything. Suddenly a man born and raised in the desert needed to negotiate deals with American and British oil companies.

When it came to uniting the seven sheikhdoms in the early 1970s, Sheikh Zayed didn't have access to phones, faxes and email to communicate and make a deal with the disparate groups. He had to meet face to face with the leaders of tribes and families and come to arrangements that would work for all of them.

He also had to argue for a vision that would dramatically change the Emiratis' way of life forever. He wanted to use the wealth of oil to open up a land that had been closed for centuries, to make it a modern, internationalised state. Sheikh Zayed had convinced sceptical tribal leaders that it was in the national interest to have development on a scale and at a speed that was perhaps unprecedented.

Ultimately he achieved this through sheer force of personality. But thirty-three years on from the founding of the UAE, change had brought its own price.

One point often lost is that the Emiratis are a minority in their own land. At the time of Sheikh Zayed's death, Emiratis numbered only some 500,000 out of a population of about four million. As a consequence, the locals risked seeing their culture and their identity overrun by the glitzy influences of the west. Alcohol. Fast food. Television. The values of a permissive and godless society were suddenly on the Emiratis' very doorstep.

In historical terms, all of this massive change had happened pretty well overnight. So there was a deep concern about the loss of cultural identity and heritage that comes from moving away from traditional roots.

One of my head trainers, Rashid, is a good example of the impact of modernisation on Emirati families and the pressure it has brought to bear inside families. Rashid was born in Al Ain and grew up as a real camel man. In the 1950s and 1960s he was a camel jockey, and as a kid he would ride a camel in wedding celebrations, festivals and so on as well as at the races. It's extraordinary to think that when I was at school watching man first walk on the moon, Rashid was riding camels around the oasis.

In the space of one generation, Rashid's family went in dramatically different directions. His oldest son attended university and worked in medicine; his life has taken him away from his traditional camel roots. Rashid's second son, on the other hand, finished high school and decided to work with camels. Financially this was a good choice, because the really good camel trainers who train for the sheikhs can make a small fortune.

The pull of modernity has created tensions like this in many Emirati families. Sons have moved away from rural areas to cities like Abu Dhabi and Dubai to pursue work, others will travel to universities in the UK, the USA or Australia and become exposed to completely new cultures and ways of thinking. It's become a huge challenge for the society. Since the beginning, family and tribe have been the centre of life. Now they are both under stress.

It was entirely possible that, with the death of Sheikh Zayed, the camels might have taken a big nosedive. But they didn't. If anything, they became more and more important as a means of preserving Emirati identity. The camel had been central to the survival of the desert people. You would carry your family and all your possessions on a camel. You would sleep next to your camel. You were defined by the number of camels you possessed. Historically, without your camel, you were nothing. Now it was time to repay the debt.

There was much to do to rekindle the work of the research centre. When it was closed down, all the staff went with it, as did a good deal of the lab equipment. Now there was a new manager, a young Emirati called Mansour bin Saad. Coincidentally, Mansour's father was one of my bosses when I had first arrived in Al Ain. Mansour knew instinctively how important camels were to his society and was committed to preserving this identity. He was more progressive and more aggressive than previous managers I'd had.

I decided that I would return to camel research for just seven months of the year to give me time to continue with the HEF Foundation work as well as other camel pursuits. But that arrangement wouldn't last long. In a couple of years the work became too intense to take any break at all.

Twenty-three
A secret surprise

It was not just me who felt most at home at Al Ain. My daughter Katya, too, knew that her heart and home were in the United Arab Emirates.

Katya came to visit soon after I'd moved back and it wasn't long before she 'bumped into' Khaled. And thus a great love story that had started when the two were teenagers took a new and decisive turn.

Despite the concerns and warnings of both families, it was obvious that there was no keeping these two apart. Katya and Khaled had decided they needed to be together, and Katya let me know this was serious. And besides, she was no longer a child.

Now, at age twenty-seven, my eldest daughter faced a real dilemma. She loved Khaled, but could she take the next step? Could she marry a man from a different culture and in some ways a different universe, and contemplate the rest of her life in an adopted country where she might not be accepted? And how would Khaled's family react? Being in love was the easy part; being together in marriage appeared devilishly complicated. Katya and Khaled had to confront tremendous barriers, both official and unofficial.

Khaled was happy to eliminate one potentially major issue. He made no demand that Katya convert to Islam. Khaled's view was that Katya was a westerner and there was no need. But whatever private concessions Katya and Khaled might make in order to ease the way, none of this was going to be easy. It is highly unusual—in fact, it almost never happens—for an Emirati man to marry a western woman. And the opposite— an Emirati woman marrying a western man—is even rarer.

The coming together of two families through marriage is a major event in the life of any Emirati family. It occasionally has to do with love, but most marriages have a much more practical function. Normally they represent tribal alliances, and traditionally marriage was a means of uniting different families into a power grouping. By tradition, too, the maintenance of the tribe was the paramount consideration and, in order to survive the randomness of life in the desert, families did not permit the infiltration of outsiders. And you couldn't get much more of an outsider than Katya.

There has been more and more pressure on the traditional ways as modernity crept into the Emirates. In the face of that, the institution of marriage has remained a bastion of tradition. Family is the cornerstone of life, much more so than in the individualistic west, where the traditional concept of family is pretty well shattered. The pressure of being such a minority in one's own country also makes the institution of marriage that much more important. There is a desire to preserve the purity of the Emirati population in the face of cultural invasion.

Indeed, Katya and Khaled would need to find their way through a system which was geared to prevent a mixed marriage. First, there are financial penalties. While Emiratis are given land and a house when they marry and large sums of cash, this is denied to those in a mixed marriage. This is set out in black and white in the UAE government's official Marriage Fund book and is a way to encourage Emirati men to marry Emirati women.

By tradition, getting married involves negotiating over the size of the dowry that the bride will bring to the marriage. This can be a large amount of money, which then goes to help the husband establish a home. The risk, though, is that if things don't work out then the woman can be left in a precarious financial position. The two agreed that in this case Katya would contribute a nominal dowry.

Before the marriage it is essential for both bride and groom to undergo a blood test. This was introduced to minimise the risk of birth abnormalities as a result of intermarriage, recognised as a hazard because of the small size of the UAE's local population. When Katya and Khaled arrived for their test, Khaled received a cool reception from the Emirati woman in charge: 'What?' she admonished him. 'No Emirati women left?'

And then there's the marriage ceremony, normally carried out by a representative of the court who goes to the groom's house to complete the formalities in the presence of male members of the families. But when a foreigner is involved, the bride and groom must present themselves to the court, first for the preliminary paperwork and then for the marriage. Time after time, Katya and Khaled would front up for their appointment only for the official to be unable to see them or be suddenly called away for some mysterious reason.

In the end, Katya and Khaled overcame all these barriers and finally managed to get a court official to carry out the legalities. It was an incredibly sterile setting—the absolute opposite of what you would want for two young people so clearly in love. As the father of the bride, I was one of the witnesses. Khaled's father had unfortunately passed away and he had not yet told his mother or his wider family. His witness was a close friend of the newlyweds, a larger than life Kuwaiti businessman who gloried in the name of Lord Faleh. Lord Faleh was an extremely wealthy property developer who had shelled out a few thousand dollars to acquire the title of lord of the manor of East Beaulieu in Boreham, near Chelmsford in Essex. It didn't entitle him to sleep with any village maiden within the manor on her wedding night, as was the ancient right of the lord of the manor, but he said the title made him feel 'more English'. Certainly, the lord was always dressed in an immaculate western suit.

Normally a marriage is an occasion for massive celebrations. A well-off Emirati family might splash out hundreds of thousands of dollars on this, holding separate events for the men and the women, usually at a five-star hotel. These could be extraordinarily lavish affairs.

In our case, though, we had to settle for something more modest. Katya's sister Erica was also along for the occasion, and the five of us held a celebratory dinner at the top of Dubai's Emirates Towers. Good old Lord Faleh was kind enough to pick up the tab. Indeed, his generosity knew no bounds: he had also paid for Erica to travel first class from Australia, and he presented her with a pair of earrings that we later learned were worth tens of thousands of dollars. It seems that, though married, the lord had developed a sweet spot for young Erica.

And so it was that Katya and Khaled were married in January 2007, bringing full circle a relationship that had been running on and off for close to ten years. For my part I was happy that Katya and Khaled were husband and wife. Actually, I was proud of them. I saw the marriage of Katya and Khaled as a wonderful celebration of what is important about being human in a world where there is so much bigotry and prejudice. I savoured the moment. It showed what was possible when you open your life to new adventure and open your mind to what the world has to offer.

I wanted to give the new couple the best gift I could. At the time that was not so easy. Having only recently returned, I was still rebuilding my life out of the ashes of my foray to

Australia, so my finances weren't in the shape they had once been—and would be again soon.

In the good years I had invested in a ring for each of my girls. One featured a sapphire, the other a ruby and the third an emerald. I brought out the ring with the sapphire, which was a huge stone, and presented it to Katya as 'something blue'. I also gave the couple a fifty per cent share in two of the young camels I had acquired before leaving the UAE courtesy of Sheikh Sultan's trade-up offer. What else would a camel tragic do? It was also a good thing to give to a Mazrouei, given the family's deep desert roots and history with camels. Ultimately those babies sold for a decent price, so it turned out to be not a bad gift at all.

In truth, Katya and Khaled were hardly in need of a leg-up. Khaled already owned several properties courtesy of his well-connected family, so it wasn't as though they would be saving hard to put down the deposit on their first home. They were already enjoying a lifestyle that permitted spur-of-the-moment jaunts to Europe.

Having completed the legalities, the young couple confronted an enormous question: how to break the news to Khaled's mother, Fatima, and the wider family. In the absence of a father, Fatima would be the most acutely affected of all those caught up in Katya and Khaled's blossoming love story. It took Khaled several weeks to prepare himself for the big announcement but, in the event, Fatima was not terribly surprised. She had secretly suspected that marriage was on the cards. And it helped enormously that Fatima had known and loved Katya since schooldays.

Fatima told Khaled to leave it to her to manage the reactions of a family that had lived a noble tradition as desert people and now found their world invaded by a western interloper. She definitely had a tricky job.

Fatima's extended family is plugged deep into the history of Al Ain. A famous character in Emirati lore, her father was known as 'Emir' ('he who must be obeyed') to Sheikh Zayed, an indicator of how much respect he commanded. Emir was still alive and had four wives plus a five-year-old daughter at the time.

Maybe the toughest nut to crack would be the old Mazrouei family matriarch, Mama Dana, then in her early eighties. Mama Dana was a true desert woman, so tiny that her feet did not touch the ground when seated. She dressed from head to toe in black, with a triangular piece of shiny gold material fashioned into a beak-like mask covering her forehead and nose. This was the traditional desert burqa, which had the very practical purpose of keeping the sand out of her face. By her appearance she was a formidable proposition, the very embodiment of an old, conservative culture.

At the same time, this family had already been subjected to the comprehensive change that progress had brought to all Emirati families. Khaled's father had grown up in the oasis town of Liwa, deep in the western desert. Here, life had been as hard as it could be, with no electricity and few facilities to speak of to cope with the searing heat. As a younger man he drove buses and did odd jobs, in the days before oil was discovered. Khaled's father was much older than Fatima when they married and unfortunately died while Khaled was in his early twenties.

One generation on, Khaled had received an education in English at an international school and completed a master's degree in urban planning from the Sorbonne in Paris. He went on to get a scholarship to Harvard, studying at the John F Kennedy Centre for Governance. He is part of the generation that sees it as a duty to drive the UAE into the future with the skills of the twenty-first century.

Just imagine: forty years ago Khaled's father was making ends meet in the desert, driving a bus. He wouldn't even have known where the United States was, let alone Harvard. How does a society cope with a generational change like that? But they have.

The Mazroueis might have had every reason to put up the walls and keep Katya out. But they did the opposite. Whatever the official barriers, these have never got in the way of the Mazrouei family's affection for Katya. They opened their arms to her immediately, and the way they have treated her and accepted us since then has been extraordinary.

Twenty-four
God's will

One thing you learn as a vet is the need to show complete authority around an animal. You need to take charge. Some can do it naturally. For others it's always a battle.

So it was with some pride that I looked on as my daughter Erica grabbed a nasty, snarling stray dog by the scruff of the neck and held it stock-still as I plunged a tranquillising injection into its hindquarters. She'd shouldered aside another vet who'd gone all wobbly and was threatening to lose control of the situation. Erica, by contrast, showed no fear.

This was the first time I'd done serious veterinary work with my daughter and I could see she had the Tinson genes.

Erica was in her fourth year of studies at the University of Melbourne and was over in Al Ain on a two-week study trip a couple of years after I'd returned. I had started a program with the university, as well as with other universities in Australia, whereby students could travel to Al Ain and get the kind of practical experience that was not possible in Australia. Erica was the first.

There was plenty to be done. I was working with a local animal charity trying to do something about the hundreds of stray dogs and cats roaming the streets of Al Ain. The answer was simple: desex the animals or, in some cases, and regrettably, put them to sleep if they were too badly injured.

I established a mobile clinic to go around the streets and to homes. And this was where things had become tricky with the dog. If you are on a dog's territory, it thinks it is in charge. That's why it's so much easier to perform these operations in a clinic, with a trained nurse around you to keep the animal under control.

It might sound mundane compared to tangling with chimpanzees and cheetahs, but the practical work of desexing and carrying out minor surgery on cats and dogs is important in developing a young vet's skills. I'd had plenty of opportunity to do it, but in the thirty years since I'd done my studies, things had changed at university. Due to the objections of animal rights groups, it had become impossible to hone basic skills on live animals, even though they were destined for euthanasia at the RSPCA.

I could see that Erica had excellent technical knowledge. She just needed the practice. And here she and other young vets would be able to carry out dozens of surgeries in a week, as much as they might in a year in Australia. This was a great way for Erica to get a taste for perhaps becoming a desert vet, too.

Then out of the blue came a job that neither of us was prepared for.

■ ■ ■

There had been an outbreak of foot and mouth disease in the UAE and it had hit the native animals hard. The gazelles, in particular, were seriously at risk, and I needed to visit them urgently at Sheikh Sultan's farm, about an hour and a half away from Al Ain, between Abu Dhabi and Dubai.

I headed out with Erica. As we drove through the security gates and along the roadway to the sheikh's home, we got a sense of the scale of the problem. There weren't just one or two gazelles here, as you might find in a zoo: the sheikh had two thousand of these creatures, roaming freely across a vast expanse of sandy flatlands.

Arabian gazelles are gorgeous animals. They hold a special place in the history of the area. Abu Dhabi, for example, literally means 'father of the gazelle'. Sleek and slender, they hardly weigh anything, maybe only fifteen kilos or so. They have a beautiful two-toned coat, with fawn on their back, neck and head while their belly and behind are pure white. Their coat is short and glossy, to reflect the sun's radiation. In other words, they are perfectly adapted to their environment. And that was the problem.

Having evolved in the isolation of the Arabian Gulf, Arabian gazelles simply aren't built to cope with imported diseases. Foot and mouth is, of course, serious for cattle and sheep, though not necessarily deadly. They get a high fever for two or three days and will then get blisters in the mouth and on the feet. The danger is that these blisters rupture and make the animals lame. For gazelles, though, the foot and mouth virus can be devastating. It can inflame the heart tissue, leading to cardiac lesions, and they simply drop dead.

The foot and mouth virus had probably been blown in by the wind. It is incredibly infectious, so there was a need to move fast in case it devastated the entire herd.

Foot and mouth is unknown in Australia, so this was something new for Erica. I had some experience fixing minor ailments with gazelles, but nothing on this scale. There is a foot and mouth vaccine, but it's useless once an outbreak is underway.

And anyway, how do you catch them? If a gazelle is well,

you can't get within a bull's roar of it. A gazelle runs like the wind, with speeds of up to sixty-five kilometres an hour. And this presented the same challenges as I'd had with the sheikh's oryx: if you chase a gazelle or an oryx for more than five minutes and put them under stress, their muscles break down and they die. They are not physiologically equipped for long chases, because that never happens in the wild.

Our first task was to isolate the affected animals, immobilise them and take their blood for testing. We put plastic around our boots and gloved up before moving from animal to animal. It was clear which ones were already sick. Part of the job was to confirm the diagnosis by taking blood or skin scrapings, for analysis later.

We did our best by isolating those we knew were infected but we lost a quarter of the gazelles over a two-week period during this outbreak. That's the thing about being a wild animal vet: it's exciting work, but can also be incredibly frustrating. You have to have different skills for different species. The episode with the gazelles reminded me of my trials and tribulations at the Lion Safari Park as a young vet. With wild animals, like a lion or a tiger, just catching them is hard enough. Handling them is also difficult. In fact, it's all stressful; everything you do is a drama.

The sheikh appreciated that we had done all we could, but in the end he accepted it as God's will that the animals should die. There wasn't much we could do about it.

■ ■ ■

Because of the large-scale migration of wild animals from Africa, India and other parts, animals in the UAE are subject to all sorts of horrible diseases that you will virtually never find in Australia. Sometimes they're not easy to spot, and they represent a serious occupational hazard for a vet.

The most dangerous camel disease for humans goes by the grand name Crimean–Congo haemorrhagic fever. As its name suggests, it is found mainly in two parts of the world, Eastern Europe and Africa. The disease is carried by ticks found on camels, though the animals themselves are completely unaffected. For humans it is a severe, deadly disease that is only one step down from ebola. Basically, your blood vessels break down, you bleed out and you turn into a big lump of jelly. In one two-year period, nineteen animal workers in the UAE died from this, though thankfully none at our camel camps.

During our early years in Al Ain there was a prohibition on putting any animal down, even if it was in terrible and incurable suffering, because of a strong religious belief that only God could decide if a living thing should die. The exception to this rule was where it involved rabies, a killer disease that does not exist in Australia. I discovered the risk early in the piece when I was called out to a camp to deal with a camel that was very clearly suffering the 'furious' form of rabies. This is the rabid-dog kind, where an animal is running around literally out of control and typically looking to bite another animal.

Any mammal can get rabies, but in the case of camels it is very difficult to deal with. Camels are big, strong beasts and pretty well impossible to control when they are running and kicking at will. I dealt with a few cases in the early days and it was scary. You had to get hold of them using ropes and a team of helpers and euthanase them without getting in contact with saliva, and without being bitten. Then you had to remove their brain and have it sent away to confirm that it was rabies.

There's another form of rabies, though, that it is much harder to spot in a camel. Indeed, the animal looks anything but furious. I've dealt with a small number of these, where the animal had facial paralysis and was drooling, looking for all the world as though it had something stuck in its throat.

This is 'dumb' or paralytic rabies. I learned quickly to take the precaution of always putting on surgical gloves whenever I was going to stick my hand in a camel's mouth, just in case.

Dumb or furious, ninety-nine per cent of the time rabies will kill a human being if you don't get treatment straightaway. The problem is it can take weeks before any clinical symptoms of rabies appear and then it is too late. You will die. So I make sure anyone working closely with our camels is vaccinated.

Erica's experiences in the UAE exposed her to eventualities she might never encounter in Australia, yet they were invaluable for her knowledge. One lesson was the need to be constantly vigilant.

After working together on surgeries and embryo transfers for a couple of weeks, Erica concluded that I was a bit old school and a lot stubborn. She was probably right on both counts.

Twenty-five
Blood ties

Four years after she married Khaled, Katya gave birth to a baby boy who they named Hazza, my first grandchild. Because of camels I was already on very good terms with two of Khaled's uncles, both of them mad camel men. But the birth was the superglue that really brought our two families together, the Tinsons and the Mazroueis. It was a transformative event: that day all barriers disappeared and I became linked through blood to my adopted home.

Fatima had used all her influence to make sure Katya got the best possible care at the local hospital. She was unstoppable in getting what she wanted for her daughter-in-law.

After the birth I arrived to find that Fatima had set up camp and spread out her own bedding in Katya's private room so she could sleep on the floor, a very traditional Bedouin custom. So from day one the relationship between Emirati grandmother, Australian mother and Emirati–Australian child was incredibly tight. How many mothers-in-law do you know who would camp out on a hospital floor?

When you bring together two very different cultures there's always going to be some collisions, especially when it comes to how you raise a baby. Upon leaving the hospital Katya insisted there would need to be a proper baby capsule in the car. But Fatima wanted to hold Hazza in her arms while they drove away, which was the custom for Emiratis. As a good western mother, Katya had a strict daily routine for Hazza and wanted him in bed and asleep by seven o'clock. Emirati kids, on the other hand, are normally up and about with the family until all hours, basically until they drop.

But Fatima could see that Katya was good at managing Hazza. She respected her for it and backed Katya on pretty well everything to do with raising the baby. For others in the extended family such changes were something of a shock. When the old matriarch of the Mazrouei family, Mama Dana, came up to visit from her traditional home out in the Liwa sands, she was horrified to find that Hazza was already asleep. At eighty-five years of age, Mama Dana had seen generations of Emirati babies enter the world and was accustomed to having the children up and part of the family until midnight if possible.

Mama Dana liked to come and visit this unusual baby. There's a photo that sums up in one frame the true extraordinariness of the marriage. It shows the small, wizened figure of Mama Dana swallowed in a huge armchair with her feet nowhere near the ground, and Hazza sitting on her lap, taking in this old desert woman with her traditional 'beak' face-covering. What could he be thinking?

A lot of things are thrown up in unprecedented situations like these, but I tried not to overthink it. It turns out that, with goodwill, most humans can give and take and make things work.

In the early years there was a difference of opinion over the question of a car seat for Hazza, after he outgrew his baby capsule. While car seats are legally required in Australia, in the Emirates it is not unusual to see two, three or four kids roaming around the inside of a car without any restraint as they hurtle along at 120-plus kilometres an hour. There have been some horrendous deaths as a result and this was a cultural battle Katya wasn't going to lose. By and large though, there were no major clashes beyond that.

I try to spend as much time as possible with Hazza, and one of the wonderful things about being the grandfather is that I've been brought closely into all the celebrations, like birthdays, where I am invited along with all the women of the extended family.

Hazza might be Emirati–Australian, but really he was being raised as an Emirati child. As his grandfather, I would be on hand for the traditional Emirati milestones of Hazza's early years. This was important, because I felt it was my job to be part of educating Hazza in the Bedouin ways. For example, there was the occasion of fitting out Hazza in his first *dishdasha*, the white robes which Emirati males wear every day.

I bought Hazza his first toy practice rifle, which has a very different meaning to a toy gun for an Australian child. An Emirati boy needs to learn how to throw a rifle high into the air with a spinning action and then catch it cleanly as it comes back down. This harks back to the desert days when young men would be armed with the heavy colonial-era Martini-Henri rifles. Nowadays they are used ceremonially at weddings or national celebrations. There are traditional gun-dancing competitions and as a kid you are expected to be able to perform.

Hazza also needed to learn the tradition of dancing with a camel stick, a thin, hooked cane used for keeping a camel in line or hooking goods down from the top of a camel. Young Emirati males dance together in lines, using the stick as a prop. This, too, is a cultural skill Hazza needed for weddings and other celebrations.

Yet Hazza is very much a product of the new internationalised generation of Emiratis. Along with learning the traditional

Emirati ways, he has seen a lot of the west. His father, Khaled, speaks English perfectly, so Hazza has grown up with Arabic and English in the home. Hazza speaks English at school, but when the older members of the extended family come around they speak Arabic. Indeed, the concern with Hazza, as for so many Emirati children, is that English is his go-to language and that his Arabic might not be good enough for communicating with the older generation.

And along with the *dishdasha*, the ceremonial gun and the camel stick, I am just as likely to see Hazza wearing a Star Wars T-shirt and a pair of cool sunglasses, thumping away on a computer tablet.

Of course, I have taken a keen interest in Hazza's camel-riding abilities. As much as I can, I take him out to the camel camps to spend time in the meet-and-greet room, the *majlis*, that are so much a cornerstone of Gulf Arab life and where I have spent many hours of my professional life. I've learned that, for all the success we've had because of science, ultimately it is the trust built through relationships that really counts. If I could introduce Hazza to this dimension of Bedouin living then all the better.

It's here in the backblocks of the desert and away from the cities that you see the old Arabia, still operating and still very much part of the fabric of life. The word *majlis* literally means a place where you sit. It is set up with low, cushioned seating, all joined up and arranged against the walls, leaving a large open area in the middle of the room. Thus you can talk to those on the left or right of you or those opposite.

This is a place where the camel men gather and talk, often for hours at a time. They might be locals or they might drift in from up-country. Visitors from Oman or Saudi Arabia, young men and old, they're all welcome. Upon taking a seat, dates and coffee or tea will be offered. There might be a television in the corner and some people might fiddle on a mobile phone, but the *majlis* is all about the talk. If you think about the way the Bedouin related to each other in the old days, everything was about stories. Turning up out of the desert after days of seeing no-one, the first question would be, 'What's the news?'

The conversations might not be about camels at all. Maybe it's the problems you're having with your kids. Maybe someone's heard word of a new development going on. A lot of the time it is just yahoo-ing and funny stories, trading jokes and jibes. This is where I was nicknamed 'Abu Sala', 'father of baldness', in honour of my follicular challenges. In return I labelled one of my sparring partners 'Abu Kalam', 'father of words', in honour of his talkative ways. There's not much that is politically correct about banter in the *majlis*. It is very much a men's zone.

At lunchtime the host will lay on an extravagant platter of rice and lamb or even baby camel, garnished with nuts and with perhaps some vegetable curry and yoghurt thrown in. You sit on the floor and dig in with your hand.

Here in the *majlis*, enduring bonds are made. Trust is built. Men are measured. This is the soul of Arabia. There might be a Starbucks on every corner, where young Emiratis also sit and talk, but the *majlis* remains as relevant as ever as a preserve of the manners and formalities that dictate so much interaction in the Emirates.

■ ■ ■

One of the most important roles I can play as grandfather is to help create a network of support for the future for Hazza. There is a very special term for this in Arabic. It is *wasta* and it's one of the most important things a family can do for a child. *Wasta* has the sense of 'connections' and loosely translates into 'clout' or 'who you know'. The west likes to think it has evolved to a point where it is not who you know that counts but what you know. Up to a point that is true, and it is possible to rise from a log cabin to the White House. Yet even in the egalitarian west, the connections of the old school tie are still relevant.

In the Emirates, who you know matters greatly. And if I can help Hazza in this through my camel connections in some small way, then that is what I will do. That means making an effort to take Hazza along to functions with the sheikhs. I'm doing the job of the Emirati grandfather, helping to position him.

Me being a westerner and the grandfather of an Emirati child has been confusing, it must be said, for some of the locals. On one occasion Hazza came with me to a gathering after a successful day at the camel races. It was a quintessentially Gulf Arab occasion. There were poetry recitals, where men would stand unbidden in the middle of the *majlis*, turn to the sheikh and deliver poems extolling the achievements of the camels and honouring the sheikh for owning such magnificent beasts. All the while Hazza was running around the room, hiding chocolates, and generally making mischief.

Later, Sheikh Sultan was introducing Hazza to a visiting member of the Saudi royal family. There was little Hazza in his *dishdasha*, which made sense to the esteemed guest. What didn't make sense was me, standing next to Hazza in my usual shirt, jacket and pants. The Saudi royal looked at Hazza, looked at me, then did one of the biggest double takes I've ever seen. Sheikh Sultan explained that Hazza was a *mahajinat*, the Arabic word for a mixed breed camel.

Put like that, it was suddenly clear. Always back to the camels!

Twenty-six
Beauty and the beast

Here's a question for you: what makes a camel beautiful?

After twenty years of working day in and day out on ways to make a camel faster, this was a question I had never contemplated. Now my boss, Sheikh Sultan, had come up with a new challenge. Plans were underway to stage the first-ever camel beauty contest in the Arabian Gulf. This was a whole new way of celebrating the importance of the camel.

The sport of camel racing was undoubtedly a macho contest. It was a straight-out competition of speed, strength and endurance, with the animal acting as a proxy for age-old rivalries. But the beauty contest was something different. This was about the gentler side of the relationship between Bedouin and camel.

Of course, most people find very little of beauty in a camel. But if you live and breathe them, you do. The Bedouin have always had a sense of what makes one camel more appealing than another, much as people have with horses. So to that extent, the idea of measuring a camel by its looks wasn't a recent invention.

If anyone can appreciate the nuances of the camel, it is the Gulf Arabs. There are reputedly a thousand names for a camel in Arabic. There's a word to cover all sorts of eventualities and types of behaviour, including 'a female camel that doesn't drink from the watering hole when it's busy, but waits and observes'. Another is 'a bull camel that has completed the period of becoming ready to be bred, as demonstrated by his swelled belly'. Yet another is 'a female camel that walks ahead of the rest by a long distance so that it appears to be fleeing'.

In some ways the advent of the beauty contest showed a maturing of the society—it had evolved from the ancient days where you relied on a camel for survival, and Gulf Arabs now prized the camel for its sheer aesthetics.

Sheikh Sultan was captivated by this new form of showcasing the camel, as were several members of the Mazrouei family. So there was no escaping my professional life taking yet another turn. As well as breeding for speed, now I would be breeding for beauty, too. This new challenge came at the right time as I had begun to think I had reached the limits of how science could be applied to the camel.

Since producing the first calf from embryo transfer and the first calf from a frozen embryo, we had undertaken ever more sophisticated work. This had enabled us to know the sex of an embryo through biopsy and to produce identical twins from a surgically split embryo. At about the time beauty contests came along, we had also produced the first calf from frozen semen. These might sound like Frankenstein achievements, but each gave us more options to make best use of the camel genes at our disposal.

Collectively, all these world-first achievements helped improve the camel's speed, which had increased by more than thirty per cent, quite extraordinary when you consider that in the same time there has been little or no improvement in the horse's speed.

The first camel beauty contest was staged in mid-December 2008 near Liwa, where the Mazroueis had originally hailed from, on the edge of the Empty Quarter. This is the time of the year when the weather is at its kindest. It was also timed to follow on from UAE National Day, when the entire country celebrates what it means to be an Emirati. So it was very much tied in with national identity and the renaissance of the old ways.

I drove down from Al Ain on a road that travels through the classic desert landscape of undulating dunes and sand out to the horizon. Turning off the main highway and coming over the brow of a hill, it was as though I had driven straight into the fourteenth century. Dozens of camel camps were set up in the sands. Camels had been brought from all parts of the Gulf, and outside each camp were the flags of different Gulf nations: Saudi Arabia, Kuwait, Oman and, of course, the UAE. This was a gathering of the Arabian tribes.

The camels and their owners had come in huge numbers. There were more than 25,000 camels in all and as many people. The major tribes had set up large traditional tents. Old Arabia was stretched out before me, recalling a time before arbitrary borders separated the families and tribes who roamed the desert. It was a demonstration of the irrelevance of national borders in Gulf Arabia.

Makeshift roads had been fashioned through the desert sands. There was the occasional four-wheel drive, but these were routes intended for the camel handlers, leading their teams of camels behind them.

Perhaps it was a brilliant form of marketing, dreamed up by a consultant, but it struck a chord. I could see why. This was a genuine celebration for and by the people of the deep desert. It was all dust, sand, sweat and braying animals.

Along the perimeter of the camel camps were stalls displaying rural handicrafts, run by old women covered in henna tattoos and wearing the traditional desert burqa. There were contests for the best dates from different regions. There was nothing fancy about it all, no tricks or gimmicks.

■ ■ ■

At the beauty contest I linked up with an old friend, Sheikh Diab, who had set up a very grand tent for receiving old sheikh mates. The sheikh took me to the show ring, where we took our seats in a rickety old grandstand to watch proceedings. If the United Kingdom has Crufts, the world's largest dog show, then this was the Arabian equivalent for camels.

The camels on show weren't the slim brown racing variety I'd worked with. They were the huge black Hazmi camels, which are a milking breed most commonly found in Saudi Arabia but also in the Liwa oasis. I had worked with them in the early days of the embryo transfer program, when the Crown Prince decided they should be the first surrogates we used. Back then I found them to be moody, difficult customers and I was glad not to have anything more to do with them after the initial embryo work.

In this setting, though, the Hazmi camels were something else. They had a grand bearing that lent them an air of arrogance and majesty. The Hazmi males are the Rolls Royce of beauty camels because, as I was to learn, size matters: the bigger the better.

Under the rules, it was not permitted for a camel handler to lead them into the ring. Beauty camels are trained to prance into the ring by themselves. They are raised with a baby camel as their imprinted friend and best mate. If you want the Hazmi to go anywhere, lead the baby camel and the big Hazmi will follow. They are bred to show themselves off, holding their necks and heads high as if to say, 'Check out how bloody good I look.' This camel really does have tickets on itself.

The term 'beauty contest' implies something frivolous, which this was not. Judging was done by a committee of ten experts, each of whom examined a different part of the body. Like judging an Arabian horse or a Hereford bull, they look at the length of the neck, the size of the head, the size of the ear, the shape of the eye, the formation of the eyelashes, the size of the udder, and so on. Droopy lips are important, the bigger and droopier the better.

There are lots of categories: mothers and babies; fathers and babies; individuals; different ages. And different colours—from the natural-coloured, big boofy beige ones to the most prized jet black camels. The winner of each category was given a trophy as well as a large sum of money and/or a new car. It was serious stuff.

Now I understood the dimensions of my new challenge. Our main rivals in this contest were not Dubai but the Saudi Arabian camels. In this case the prize money was even greater than for the racing camels, but for the sheikhs the prize money was secondary. It was the pride of owning the most beautiful beast in the Gulf that mattered.

Sheikh Sultan had paid the equivalent of ten million dollars for three of the most beautiful camels from Saudi Arabia. That was way more than the sort of money you would pay for a top-flight racing camel. There were two females, Marayah and Naifa, and a male called Mabrokan. All three had the attributes of a champion beauty camel: jet black (the blacker, the better), big head, big feet, large droopy lips and small ears.

On the technical side, using embryo transfer to breed for beauty is much easier than breeding for speed. If you have good-looking animals, they will produce good-looking animals. Simple. Breeding for speed involves a huge number of factors that are not nearly as easy to control. But on a practical level, dealing with the Hazmis was a nightmare. These things were so big that I had to build a special elevated metal platform to get up high enough to do the routine rectal examinations and embryo flushing.

A regular-size Hazmi can do well at a beauty contest, but the very best of them are giants. And Mabrokan was truly the biggest camel I have ever seen. Ever. He was like a T. Rex, the size of a house with a head like a dining table. He would have weighed more than a thousand kilograms compared to the three to four hundred kilograms of a racing camel. Mabrokan was so big it was close to impossible to do the most basic reproductive procedure, which begins with collecting the semen. The best technique is to use electro-ejaculation, however that means a general anaesthetic. Given Mabrokan's size, and that he was worth five million dollars, I wasn't keen on that idea should something go awry.

To make matters more complicated, Mabrokan was a real pain when it came to mating. Try as we might, he just wasn't keen on Marayah and Naifa, the beautiful black Hazmis. No, Mabrokan only ever wanted to mate with the milking camels from Pakistan, which are the real scrubbers of the camel world. We were constantly trying to find ways to increase his libido so he would perform where he was needed. The sheikh jokingly suggested we might want to try Viagra.

The short of it was that Mabrokan was a moody and temperamental so-and-so. I could see this was not going to be fun.

Twenty-seven
Business and pleasure

There are striking stories about the largesse of the sheikhs. Some are certainly apocryphal, but others are very real.

In 2008 in Dubai, Ethinam—one of the camels from our reproduction program—won her third Gold Cup in successive years as she graduated through her age groups. She was our version of Makybe Diva, three times consecutive winner of the Melbourne Cup. In honour of this, Dubai's ruler, Sheikh Mohammed bin Rashid Al Maktoum, presented our trainer with a black Bentley Continental GT, along with Dubai numberplates bearing the number '4'. The lower the number, the greater the value of the numberplate, so this was probably three times more valuable than the car itself. This was on top of the 250,000 dollars or so in prize money.

Another time at a camel race meeting in the north of the UAE, Sheikh Sultan purchased thirty-five promising young camels. They were a good acquisition for the president's herd. The cost was enormous, probably no less than twenty million dollars, and the transactions all happened in a couple of days.

In Al Ain, the senior Emiratis working on behalf of the president will snap up the fastest of the young camels competing in smaller backblocks races. They might pay around 250,000 to 300,000 dollars for a single camel, which isn't a bad take-home amount for a Bedouin trainer chancing his arm.

The camel beauty contest, too, always offers the chance for a relatively poor Bedouin to sell his pretty little camel 'up' to the sheikhs. It's a windfall for the less well-off citizens and it's also a win for the sheikh, who gets a faster or more beautiful camel. The decisions are always quick and the deal is done on a handshake. The camel changes hands immediately and the Bedouin collect their money pretty soon after.

On one level, the money around the camel races is big because the Emiratis are competitive about who has the best camel and, of course, this drives the prices up. But some families and tribes are not business-oriented and they haven't prospered as much as others from the country's oil riches. Passing the wealth around through camel racing and trading helps these tribes preserve a traditional lifestyle and values, but at the same time gives them support without the need to go begging to the sheikh for money.

This system has been a potent force in maintaining stability inside the UAE, in a region that is constantly on the boil. It is a fundamental reason the UAE has remained untroubled and untouched by the uprisings which spread across the Arab world from late 2009. Even in the post-GFC era, the camel money on offer has gone up, not down.

There is serious prize money, as well as cars, to be won, even in the more obscure meetings. In Qatar I attended a mid-level race—not even the main race—where there were 250 cars for prizes. The winner of the third-last race received a McLaren concept car. The winner of the second-last race received 600,000 dollars. For the last race, the winner took home one and a half million dollars.

As far as the sheikhs are concerned, one of the biggest threats to the camel social security system is drugs. Every time my sheikh buys a camel that has run a fantastic time, we test it to make sure it is not on EPO or some other illegal substance to increase its speed. I have also carried out drug testing at the local races, though now I am usually only involved in the big international races.

Some guys have even tried their hand at blood doping. This has produced the occasional disaster when they take the blood from one camel and inject it into another. And it threatens the fairness of the races, the chance for the little Bedouin from the desert backblocks to come up with a belter of a camel that he can sell to the sheikhs.

The sheikhs' number-one obsession these days is to try to find out what everyone is using, to find out who's cheating. The most likely offenders are the Bedouin trainers and owners, who are very well connected and have access to illegal medicines. Penalties have gone through the roof. It's no different to the Tour de France or horseracing. Drugs are more sophisticated than they were five or ten years ago. If it's being used with humans or with horses, then chances are it is being used with camels. In the 1990s the camel races were pretty much immune from this sort of thing, but now, courtesy of the internet, people with the intent can get anything from anywhere.

■ ■ ■

It took a few attempts, but before too long we achieved huge success in the camel beauty contests.

Mabrokan had proven himself too fickle when it came to the other beautiful Hazmis, so we used the services of another bull, owned by a sheikh from the western region of Abu Dhabi. The mother was Naifa, and she produced a real star called

Nazar. We had bred a few good ones, but we knew from the moment she was born that Nazar was the pièce de résistance. Even as a calf she was a giant. Her coat was jet black and all her proportions were right.

By now the Liwa beauty contest was a major Gulf event, with close to thirty thousand camels and about the same number of owners and handlers arriving from across the sands. The roadway leading to the camel show ring had been officially named 'Millionaires Road', as a nod to the money changing hands with the buying and selling of camels. If anything, the beauty contest had become bigger than the races, so again the pressure was well and truly on.

In 2012 we entered Nazar there as a young calf and she took out the title in her class. The following year Nazar went in as a yearling and won several different classes, including the prize for most beautiful baby camel. She went through to the finals to be pitted against the winners from all classes—and she did it. Nazar took out the biggest prize of all: best in show.

Upon hearing the announcement, a member of the Saudi royal family was overcome with emotion. He literally jumped out of the stands, burst into the judging ring and started reciting poetry to Nazar, in florid tribute to what an amazing animal she was. On the spot the Saudi royal offered Sheikh Sultan eight million dollars for this most beautiful specimen. He was smitten and wanted this camel bad. Sheikh Sultan knocked him back.

The Saudi royal's ardour was understandable. Nazar not only won best in show but she did it with a perfect ten out of ten, which is why I've nicknamed her Nadia, after the Romanian gymnast Nadia Comaneci who was the first to ever get a perfect score at the Olympics.

Nazar's brothers and sisters have also won a clutch of medals, but Nazar is the absolute standout. One of our embryo babies, she is both the most beautiful and the most valuable camel on the planet. With her big liquid brown eyes and long,

long eyelashes, she has the bearing of a Hollywood starlet. You half expect her to emerge from her own private caravan, with sunglasses and a list of outrageous demands. It hardly seems right that she should have to bend her neck down to scoop out feed with the others.

As it is, Nazar resides in specially built luxury stables equipped with air-conditioning to keep her coat in tip-top condition. There are two or three handlers constantly by her side, even sleeping with her at night.

■ ■ ■

The camel boys have now rechristened me 'Abu Nazar' (father of Nazar). But she can cause me more sleepless nights than any teenager. Whenever she gets sick, it's a major stress time. If she sneezes, I worry. Still.

And what of Mabrokan? Well, he met a premature end and never got to see the success of Nazar. While being fed with lucerne he developed a bout of bloat, which is common in cattle but very rare in a camel. The giant evidently became afflicted in the middle of the day and, uncharacteristically, there was no-one around to see what was happening for the first hour, even though he was meant to be under 24/7 watch. By the time the handlers realised it, Mabrokan was on death's door. And by the time the vet got to him, he was dead.

Perhaps luckily for me, I was in Rome that day. I was in the middle of lunch in a restaurant when I got the phone call telling me Mabrokan was dead. I told the vet back in Al Ain to cut out Mabrokan's testicles, take a sample of his skin and to store it all in the freezer. I thought by at least preserving parts of him we might be able to clone him later. But bellowing instructions about what to do with a camel's balls in the middle of a crowded Roman restaurant left the other patrons somewhat nonplussed, judging from the looks on their faces.

I flew back to Al Ain within twenty-four hours to help process the remains and generally get on top of what had been a big disaster. Five million dollars' worth of camel had died a perfectly preventable death, all because no-one was watching.

Mabrokan had already been dead a couple of hours before parts of him were cut out and frozen, but it was a step worth taking. In the meantime, Sheikh Sultan took his own steps to preserve Mabrokan. He decided to send his body to Paris to have him stuffed—all one thousand kilograms of him. He was then freighted back to the UAE to take up permanent residence in the sheikh's car museum.

People wonder how you could seriously have a beauty pageant for camels and, even more, how a camel could ever be valued at eight million dollars just for its looks. But Arabs probably wonder why you would put a bull in the show ring. They would say, 'Hang on, we're showing an animal worth seven million dollars—we're showing something significant, while you're showing something worth twenty thousand dollars.' That's what happens when you have people who are fanatical about an animal and have the money to match their passion.

From my point of view, the beauty camel phenomenon had been a blessing because it gave another string to my bow in a year when success was coming in spades.

Twenty-eight
The Golden Sword

At the end of the day, if you don't perform on your home turf and win the big cups and the Golden Swords in front of your boss, then it's not a good look. It took twenty-five years after first coming to Al Ain, but in 2013 everything we had worked for seemed to be finally coming together.

The 2013 carnival season had been our most successful on record. That year we won a dozen Gold Cups at races in the premier carnivals at Qatar and Dubai; twenty years previously we were overjoyed to win just one Gold Cup. Now it was the last day of the carnival season, at the end of two weeks of racing at home in Abu Dhabi.

We had bred a champion female called Theeba ('wolf'), who was performing out of her skin and had already picked up a Gold Cup at the Dubai meeting held earlier. There was a lot of expectation that today she would take the Golden Sword, which goes to the winner of the open-age female category. It is the most prestigious prize of all and is run as the final race on the final day of the carnival. The prize money is one million dirhams, the equivalent of about 300,000 dollars, but, as ever, the money hardly mattered.

The meeting was held at the Al Wathba racetrack, the same track I had come to fresh off a plane from Australia twenty-five years before. I had turned up there with no clue as to how a race was run in the Arab Gulf and had received an instant education in how their society works when the late President of the United Arab Emirates, Sheikh Zayed, arrived to an ecstatic greeting from the assembled Bedouin and sheikhs. I had watched the day unfold from a seat in a temporary tent, surrounded by Sheikh Zayed's presidential guard and with the barrel of a Kalashnikov kind-of shoved up my left nostril.

Back then Al Wathba was a single dirt track with a tent as a temporary grandstand. Now it had been developed into a massive complex. There were two separate racing tracks: a shorter one for younger camels, with a four-, five- or six-kilometre loop, and an eight-kilometre track, where we were racing today, for the adult camels. There was a huge concrete and glass grandstand, from where spectators could watch proceedings unfold in air-conditioned comfort. The entrance to the complex was arrayed with the flags of all the Gulf countries, framing large photographs of the national leaders.

Racing was now covered live for television from every conceivable angle. There was a drone beaming out pictures from overhead, camera crews followed the race from both sides of the track, and cameras were embedded in the track itself, putting viewers smack in the middle of the action. Throughout the carnival a nightly television show featured camel pundits from around the Gulf, dissecting the results of the day and offering their analysis on what the next day's racing would bring.

A gigantic photograph of the late president, Sheikh Zayed, dominated the grassed area in the middle of the track. Directly underneath the photograph of Sheikh Zayed the prizes were on display: 150 new Range Rovers, Mercedes, Lamborghinis and other luxury brands, lined up in neat rows and ready to be driven away. Next to the grandstand was the yard from where camel handlers walked their charges down to the starting blocks. There was also a VIP *majlis*, reserved as a meeting place for the senior sheikhs of Abu Dhabi, Dubai and Qatar, and off to the side of the racetrack two giant Medivac helicopters were on stand-by.

On this the final day, the Bedouin owners had arrived just after dawn, filling the car park with four-wheel drives and utes, in time for their camel races, which took up the morning schedule. After a break the afternoon session was devoted to the final three, the most prestigious races, involving the best camels owned by the sheikhs of Abu Dhabi, Dubai and Qatar. In the lead-up there were a series of special events: a military display, parachutists and a traditional local custom called the hair dance, where a troupe of women sway their heads in rhythm, swinging their hair from side to side.

When I watched my first race here twenty-five years before, there was a long wait for the main race before Sheikh Zayed arrived in his Pullman from across the desert. Now events were run more tightly.

The final race was due to start at 2pm. At 1.40 you could hear a helicopter coming in from the north and landing five minutes' drive away at a helipad. This was Sheikh Hamdan bin Mohammed, the Crown Prince of Dubai. A couple of minutes later another helicopter arrived from the west, this one bearing my boss, Sheikh Sultan.

The sheikhs were then driven from the helipad to the track, choreographed to arrive at about the same time, so they all got to shake hands and rub noses in the traditional way.

The Crown Prince of Dubai emerged from his black Mercedes four-wheel drive, with the numberplate '11', accompanied by an entourage of four or five cars. His father, Mohammed bin Rashid Al Maktoum, the ruler of Dubai, had an identical car, which carried the plate number '1'.

There was no need to announce the arrivals of the sheikhs. Everyone knew who they were from the direction their helicopters had flown in.

In the old days, when Sheikh Zayed was alive, he would bring the rulers of the seven emirates to the track for the last day. Sheikh Khalifa followed that tradition for a few years, too, along with the next tier of sheikhs. So you might have had fifty sheikhs in the grandstand, with full-on security.

But times have changed and it is now impossible for all the sheikhs to get away. Yet still the ruling families of Abu Dhabi and Dubai made sure they were there.

After the friendly introductions and warm smiles, the sheikhs returned to their cars so they could follow the race from a VIP road built on the inside of the racetrack. From now on, it was war.

The grandstand was filled with about two thousand people, mostly Bedouin but also some sheikhs. One disadvantage of the grandstand is that, while it gives you a great view of the start and the track, it is a long way from the action. After a minute or so the camels are well off into the distance, so you don't have any sense of the unfolding drama. Others took the option of piling into their cars to follow the camels at ground level, from a road on the outside of the track. This is an area about a hundred metres wide, which accommodates around two hundred utes, pickups and other assorted vehicles as they thunder along with locals hanging out the windows or popping out through the roof of their cars, screaming and yelling encouragement for their camel.

My head trainer, Rashid, was in his own four-wheel drive on yet another road built inside the track. From here he could control the tiny stainless steel robot 'jockey' strapped to Theeba's hump. The robots represented another dramatic change from the first time I had witnessed a race. In 2002, after international human rights pressure, the UAE became the first Gulf state to put a stop to the practice of using young children as jockeys.

After being sent to the UAE from poor countries like Bangladesh and Sudan, some had been injured while others had even died. It was the right thing to do, and it turned out that camels actually ran faster with the lighter weight. The robot weighs only two kilograms and is equipped with a whip, which the trainer can activate by remote control. Normally, though, the whip is hardly used. Instead, Rashid talks to the camel through a two-way on the robot. He was one of thirty trainers in control cars jostling for position to keep close to their camels.

Rashid had a camel camp about a kilometre away from the track, and I had repaired to the quiet of his *majlis* there for the big race. Only three of us were present: my chief veterinary assistant, Dr Kuhad, Rashid's oldest son, Diab, and me. For me it was more important to watch the live television coverage and get the view from all angles than to be there in person. You don't get quite the same sense of excitement and adrenalin as being trackside, but it's a lot better for getting the full picture of how the race is unfolding.

I was confident Theeba could win this race, but anything can happen on the day. And of course, other Abu Dhabi trainers and the staff from Qatar and Dubai were also determined to take out the Golden Sword.

What eventuated was one of the most extraordinary races I've ever witnessed.

■   ■   ■

The thirty or so camels were lined up ready to go behind the long barrier, essentially a thin sheet of brown plastic attached to a metal frame. At the signal a mechanical arm lifted the barrier and they thundered off.

Following them were cars on three different roadways: one

on the inside of the track for the sheikhs, another on the inside of the track for the trainers and the third on the outside for friends, family and barrackers.

It wasn't long before I started to feel very uneasy. I was looking for Theeba's colours in the throng but still couldn't see them. In the president's colours of red augmented with gold trim, which was Rashid's signature, she should have been obvious. But out in front from the start were the camels with black and white saddlecloth, the colours of the ruler of Dubai.

For the first seven minutes we simply could not see Theeba or hear the commentator call her name. As usual, the cameras also panned right back from the leader, yet we still couldn't see her. The three of us wondered where in heaven's name she was. Even other Abu Dhabi camels were well ahead of her, if she was still in the race at all.

At the seven and a half minute mark, something very odd occurred. A bright orange camel, which had been sitting at the rear of the race, suddenly made an appearance in the leading group. We didn't recognise this orange camel, but it was going like a missile. She came from at least five or six hundred metres behind.

Then it dawned on us: this was Theeba. It seemed Rashid, had been so confident she would win that he had applied henna to her from head to toe *before* the race began. I had never seen this done. Trainers will sometimes henna the lower legs as a good luck charm, but Rashid had hennaed the whole camel. Unbelievable.

From then on Theeba came charging through, overtaking every other camel as if they were standing still. By the ten-minute mark she was in front and then she found another burst of speed. She took the race by a hundred metres and in the process set a record time of twelve minutes and four seconds over eight kilometres.

The three of us in Rashid's *majlis* were jumping up and down like little kids in excitement, over the moon that Theeba had won. The race was finished. The season was finished. We had won the Golden Sword. Within minutes Rashid's *majlis* was inundated with literally thousands of people. Every car, man and his dog headed over from the racetrack to congratulate Rashid. It seemed like almost every Abu Dhabi local was there, from the sheikh down, rubbing noses and shaking hands with the trainer and the sheikh. And so it went for a couple of hours.

Theeba's win capped a meeting where we won ten of the sixteen Gold Cups up for grabs, my head trainer winning the bulk of them. We'd taken out the Golden Sword and smashed the track record. That all this happened in our home town of Abu Dhabi made it all the sweeter.

The achievement was commemorated in a special photo showing the Golden Sword and all the gold cups we'd collected over the 2013 season. In the middle of the photograph was the president, Sheikh Khalifa, with the Crown Prince of Abu Dhabi, Sheikh Sultan and the uncles. It captured the centre of power in the UAE. In twenty-five years, this was the first time such an official photograph was taken and then published in the national press.

If we could have taken the same photo in 2014 it would have displayed double that number of Gold Cups and Golden Swords. But to me that photo is the breakthrough moment and it represents the pinnacle of success. It holds a special significance, too, because it is one of the last public photos of Sheikh Khalifa, the man who had employed me for over twenty-five years.

I keep it next to our first Gold Cup photo taken in 1996, a photo in which we look extraordinarily young and are boasting one lousy trophy. It's a reminder that back then we weren't even in the race, let alone competing.

Twenty-nine
A rich life

The year 2013 marked the twenty-fifth anniversary of the Hilli Embryo Transfer Centre. When I arrived with Heath Harris and the boys, the camels used to trot for half the race and then slow down, until finally they walked across the line; we used to dream that a camel might even canter the whole way through, let alone gallop. In the league table of camel racing, we ranked well down the list.

In that time we have improved the speed of the camel from an average of thirty kilometres an hour to an average of forty-three kilometres an hour. A drone has even measured a camel doing a top speed of fifty kilometres an hour in the last half kilometre of the race—this is its over-the-line speed after galloping for eight kilometres. The lesson is that if you keep selectively breeding for speed, then a remarkable change occurs.

From an idea in the desert, the camel research centre has been developed virtually into a university, with some sixty lab and technical staff. On the way through we have pioneered five world firsts in camel breeding: they are the first birth of an embryo transfer calf; the first calves from frozen embryos; the first identical twin camel calves; the first pre-sexed embryo calves; and the first reported frozen calf using frozen semen and artificial insemination. It's easy to reel these off now, but behind each has been years of thinking and sheer hard work.

We still only have around 3500 camels but, boy, are they something. We consistently win the biggest races. And it might only get better.

We have done a lot of work recently on techniques for freezing semen. This will come into play with our IVF research for what I consider to be the next frontier: producing superior milking camels.

The camel milk industry has been taking off. Again, it is an example of finding a new role for an ancient part of the culture. In the swish cafés of the UAE, patrons can now order up a camelcino to go. Historically, camel milk sustained the Bedouin when food was scarce. It is rich in vitamins and nutrients and is lower in cholesterol than cow's milk. So there is great scope for milking camels to help populations in poorer countries as well as in the west, where there is a growing demand for its medicinal qualities. It has much higher levels of Vitamin C than cow's milk and is considered by some to have an insulin effect, making it beneficial for people with diabetes.

■ ■ ■

I have many reasons to thank Heath Harris for finding me in the Australian outback that day in 1988, but this is perhaps the greatest: it has allowed me to cross the boundaries of race and religion, and create a life full of rich possibility. And not just for me, but for my family as well.

The passport of our youngest daughter, Madeline, records

her place of birth as Al Ain, United Arab Emirates. That's something she's proud of. Whenever she flew over to visit me from her home with Patti in Florida, people would ask her where she was from. 'From here,' she would reply. 'I'm from Al Ain.'

Almost thirty years ago I came to a young country where everything was possible. I was given a blank sheet of paper and the opportunity to write my own story, and I'd like to think I have also made a contribution to the way the UAE has changed. I know the country has changed me.

Since Hazza, Katya and Khaled have had two more children, a girl called Mahra and a boy called Zayed. So I have become a grandfather to three Emirati children. Being linked by blood to an Emirati family has brought me acceptance in a close-knit, somewhat closed society. After more than twenty years, this was the moment when I finally went from being an outsider to an insider. Since then everything has changed. It has given me a new status in the society. Now I am more likely to be introduced to other Emiratis as 'Jed Hazza', meaning the grandfather of Hazza, rather than Dr Alex, the camel vet.

I had always enjoyed the cordial respect of the locals, both because of my work with the camels and because I have stayed so long while others come and go, but being linked by blood has given me a unique status and taken that respect to a new level. I am generally treated more like a local. It is as though I have been brought under the camel security blanket, like the Bedouin.

I have five of my own camels being looked after out at a camel camp. They might become champions or they might not, but it's fun having my own in the racing game. The sheikhs have already bought some of my camels, and maybe one day a sheikh will buy these ones. Or I might trade them for others.

Becoming part of the society makes me feel like a different person. I'm not making selfish decisions because I want to make a quick killing and get out of here, like most people do. Having a blood link to the Emiratis means I think years ahead.

This has given me a financial freedom I could never have imagined. In Dubai not so long ago, I picked up a Ferrari, in memory of my father. Dad was the most honest man in the world and would never have dreamed of spending a cent on such luxury. His one rush of blood was to buy a red Holden Monaro with black racing stripes, but he always said he was waiting for the day his superannuation came through so that he could buy a really flash car. Unfortunately Dad passed away before that happened, however I was now in a position where I could afford to buy the Ferrari and so I did it. I dedicated it to Dad and the idea of living for the moment.

I have also bought a house in Cuba, which I can escape to every so often. I had always wanted to find an old Edwardian house in Australia to restore; I happened to find such a house, but it's in Cuba. And it allows me to indulge my Hemingway fantasies.

I've also been able to pass the wealth around to those who've helped me so much in the past. People like our old Sri Lankan maid, Kanthi, who looked after our children when they were growing up. In her case I've been able to get her through some tough times, when it looked like she might lose her home in Sri Lanka.

Some of my friends have remained vets their whole lives. Nothing wrong with that, so have I, but because of the huge changes in the UAE I have had the great good fortune to be able to reinvent myself and put myself into situations where I am continually stimulated. This is the only place I could have done it.

The camels have provided a universal language that has helped me to break through political barriers to give assistance to people who need it. Through the HEF Foundation I have been able to get into everywhere, from Mongolia to Rajasthan, and even to sanctions-bound Iran, where I stood in front of a massive photograph of Ayatollah Khomeini and lectured students at Tehran University. Looking into the audience, to my surprise most of the vets in training were women.

Some of my vet friends have now retired, but I don't want to. It's not about money any longer, it's just that I enjoy what I'm doing. Besides, now I am utterly comfortable in what was once a totally alien environment, with rules and protocols I could barely comprehend.

The first time I ventured into a *majlis* I was terrified. There were guns everywhere, and I had no idea how to deal with personal space. Should I shake hands or not? Sometimes I'd be walking with a sheikh and he would grab me by the hand. I learned that it was like dealing with the Queen: you can't touch her, but if she touches you, fine. Now I've been going to sheikh functions for so long that some of my stories have become folklore, so when a new person comes to the *majlis* they'll introduce me and use one of my stories, maybe from twenty years ago.

Will I ever return to Australia to live? I doubt it. It's hard for me to do what I do anywhere else but this corner of the world.

At my present home I have assembled a new collection of pets: a bulldog called Winnie, a snake, a chameleon and two rainforest frogs, which are the best low-maintenance pets you can have. They survive on baby mice and cockroaches, which is quite handy.

The chameleon is truly the most extraordinary animal I've ever had anything to do with. I've called him Spock, because his hands have two fingers splayed out in a big V. He is difficult to take your eyes off, with his eyes rotating independently at a hundred miles an hour, while the rest of him remains perfectly still. Most animals are designed to make a getaway using speed, but the chameleon just disappears into the background and you wouldn't know where he was. If you wear a pink shirt, he starts going pink. You can, by the way, still get chameleons at pet shops in the UAE, but it helps that I have a mate at the local zoo who is a dealer.

I am certain that living in a Muslim society has helped me come to terms with losing our two babies. The all-encompassing philosophy of Islam is that whatever happens is God's will. There is a pervasive sense that you, as a mere mortal, cannot control your destiny or the destiny of your children. This 'no blame/no responsibility' approach can allay the guilt and the questions that can plague you in the dark times. If I can't control what happens around me then, you might say, it is easier to surrender to my fate and move on.

Yet I have had many dark moments, when I couldn't stop thinking about the two girls we have lost. My friends tell me that when asked how many kids I have, I will occasionally answer 'five'. It never quite goes away, but now I find myself thinking how lucky we are to have three girls alive and doing so well. They live on different continents, with Katya in the UAE, Erica in Australia and Maddy in the USA, where she and her husband Jake have a baby girl, Katie. That makes grandchild number four. All my daughters are out in the world, which is a good place to be. And, courtesy of Erica, the Tinson bloodline of vets continues.

In the end, I have made good on my pact with myself to live a big life, like my Dad. And it's all because I said yes to adventure.